100 Passengers

100
Passengers

MARGARET D. Mitchell

WINEPRESS **WP** PUBLISHING

WinePress Publishing (PO Box 428, Enumclaw, WA 98022) functions only as book publisher. As such, the ultimate design, content, editorial accuracy, and views expressed or implied in this work are those of the author.

Unless otherwise noted, all Scriptures are taken from the Holy Bible, New International Version, Copyright © 1973, 1978, 1984 by the International Bible Society. Used by permission of Zondervan Publishing House. The "NIV" and "New International Version" trademarks are registered in the United States Patent and Trademark Office by International Bible Society.

The stories are all true, though most of the names have been changed.

ISBN 1-57921-788-5
Library of Congress Catalog Card Number: 2005901738

Dedications

I dedicate this book
to the
Father, Son, and Holy Spirit.

He said to them, "Go into all the world and preach the good news to all creation."

—Mark 16:15

Prologue

God spoke to me in February 2001 to write a book and title it *100 Passengers*. I remember His instructions very clearly. I was driving home from church one afternoon. My lungs filled with air and my heart pounded as I heard the Holy Spirit's words resound in my mind. My first prayer response was, "What?!" Then a series of questions raced through my consciousness: What do You want this book to be about? Fiction or non? How long should it be?

As with many endeavors God leads us to, He didn't answer me right away. Instead, He revealed His *how* and *what* and *why* along the way. Weeks and several chapters passed before I recognized that the book I was writing, via the Holy Spirit, was a retrospective of divine appointments that God orchestrated between passengers and me in airports and on airplanes.

God always awed me in this process. He chose the trips, places, times, and people. As His surprises and revelations unfolded, my trust and faith in Him increased. And so did my prayer repertoire. He grew me aboundingly in a short amount of time. Through this journey, we became a very close team, with Him leading me into unexplainable circumstances that would, at times, bring me to my knees. As His divine plan overtook me, I reveled in spending hours alone with God, writing, communing, weeping, and de-lighting in His presence. Throughout, He was very sweet to me, giving me signs of encouragement along the way.

When I shared with passengers that God orchestrated a preordained meeting between them and me, many of them cried in relief. I was amazed at how people would, within seconds, open up and share their struggles, many of which had been held in secrecy until these precious moments arrived. Often, I would wonder whether they had anyone else to pray for them. I learned that, in many cases, they did not.

I knew that God led me to this job as a flight attendant more than sixteen years ago. What I didn't understand then was why. But now I do. Initially, God used this job of physically serving others—food, drink, and even pick-ing up trash—to humble me into a true servant of His. Although I was resistant at first, I wasn't too resistant for Him. I came to this job arrogant, full of self, thinking I was too educated to do this kind of work. But God had a plan for me. Although it didn't seem like a very good one to me in the beginning, I chose to go along with it anyway.

Over the years, God created space in my heart for hu-mility, mercy, and love. Throughout this journey, God empowered me to do His work of serving others His way. To that end, I came to know God's peace, joy, and favor unspeakable in my workplace. And I understood His true meaning of the word steward(ess).

To the 100 passengers
who flew on my flights
who knew such pain
who knew such plight
who lost loved ones
along the way
who cried
and mourned
and ached
and prayed
that God would bring a brighter day
that God would show His mighty grace.
Please grant them peace
and strength
and love.
O let them see Your face above
the darkness,
bitterness,
sin,
the fall.
O thank You, Jesus
for Your call.

Chapter I

But he said to me, "My grace is sufficient for you, for my power is made perfect in weakness." Therefore I will boast all the more gladly about my weaknesses, so that Christ's power may rest on me.

—2 Corinthians 12:9

During my first five years as a stewardess, my employer experienced five airplane crashes. On a particular trip during this season, I was assigned to work the same route as an airplane that had crashed a week prior. I was the stewardess in charge.

The customer gate agent who was assigned to this flight informed me that the majority of passengers who were about to board were family members of those who had died in this latest crash. The agent also informed me that one passenger would be brought down early because she was so distressed.

My legs and hands trembled at this news. I felt completely unprepared to receive these people. I was still recovering myself, fearful that I could be next in line to crash. I said a quick, silent prayer asking God to strengthen me. Then I stood at the airplane entrance and anticipated the first passenger's arrival.

As I peered up the Jetway, I saw the woman stagger around the corner. She was so overcome with grief that she could not walk straight. When she saw our airplane, she immediately wailed. Her cries echoed all the way down the metal loading bridge, straight into my heart. Although I had been a Christian since my teens, I felt so inadequate, and I knew that only God could comfort her in this moment of grief.

When she reached the threshold of the airplane, she grabbed it with both hands. Her large body quivered. She then looked up at the crack of sky between the Jetway and the airplane, and, with her fingers still grasping the aircraft doorjamb, she cried out to God in a language that was known only to Him.

I could barely fight my own tears. I prayed silently and repeatedly for God to show me what to do. Since my job was to receive many distressed people, I knew that falling apart was not an option.

After a moment, I put my arm around the woman. She took a deep breath and reached for my hand. "Thank you, honey," she said through her sobs. I glanced at the woman's boarding pass and led her down the aisle. I pointed out her seat and handed her a box of tissues, all the while praying, "God, what would You have me do?"

Immediately after I returned to the front of the aircraft, the remainder of the passengers boarded. One by one, their somber faces silently passed before me. And with each one, I felt deep sorrow. I looked down to see that they carried shopping bags, brimming with funeral flowers. In the midst of my overwhelming feelings, I noticed that the pungent aroma of those flowers quickly permeated the cabin. And I knew then that I would forever remember God's amazing grace and the bittersweet scent of a hundred passengers.

"To him who overcomes and does my will to the end, I will give authority over the nations—"
—Revelation 2:26

One day, a customer agent approached our aircraft and informed me that he was about to board a teenage runaway. Although, up to this point, I had worked my share of flights in which juveniles and criminals were transported, they had always been accompanied by some type of law enforcement authority. This young man would be traveling alone.

I expressed my concerns about transporting the teen without marshals. The agent attempted to assure me that all would be fine, saying that the authorities that had brought the teen to the gate insisted that he was just returning home and would behave obediently. The agent added that authorities would meet our flight at our destination and that they would escort the teen home. I wasn't convinced, and I had no peace about the situation. Reluctantly, I received the young man on the airplane. With this, we closed the aircraft door and took off for Charlotte.

When we arrived, there were no authorities to meet us. I escorted the teen up the Jetway to turn him over to our gate agents until they arrived. However, once we got to the top of the Jetway and the boy saw that no authorities were in sight, he ran. I immediately kicked off my high heels and sprinted down the concourse after him. Crowds parted, and agents' radios buzzed as we streamed passed.

Suddenly, the boy took a turn through an emergency exit door, which set off alarms. I followed him through the door, down a flight of stairs, and out onto the tarmac. I immediately felt the prickly cement rip my stockings. Just as we ran past the nose of an airplane, several baggage tractors converged upon him. The drivers had been notified via radio. They circled around the teen, and with nowhere else to run, he dropped to his knees in surrender.

I immediately halted and looked down at the boy, who was several feet ahead of me and completely vulnerable. I gasped for breath, and my heart pounded with sadness. "What was so unbearable at home that this boy would take this kind of risk?" I wondered. "Does he know God at all?" I couldn't bear to see him restrained, so I said a short prayer for him before I turned and walked away. As I headed back up the stairs to the concourse, I felt convicted concerning my own secret shackles of fear and pain. Like this boy, I wanted to keep running. Like him, I knew it was time to surrender fully. So I stopped for a moment in that empty stairwell, held onto the rail, and examined the holes in my stockings. There, I saw a reflection of my soul. Then I asked Jesus to help me, just as I had asked Him to help the boy.

Chapter 3

But in your hearts set apart Christ as Lord. Always be prepared to give an answer to everyone who asks you to give the reason for the hope that you have. But do this with gentleness and respect . . .

—1 Peter 3:15

While I received passengers one day, a woman walked slowly down the aisle toward me. I sensed that something was wrong from her forlorn face and slow movement. I met her halfway to help her with her bag and to show her to her seat. The woman thanked me and immediately asked for a cocktail. I informed her of the airline's policy to serve alcohol after takeoff. She wedged her body into a seat and looked up at me. "I just lost my husband," she said.

Stunned, I replied, "I'll make it a double." I turned and headed to the galley, where I mixed a concoction of Jack Daniels and Coke. When I handed the woman the drink, she shared that she was on her way home to bury her husband's body, which was situated in the cargo bin below. I was speechless.

After takeoff and a drink service, the woman asked me to sit with her. "Help me, God," I silently prayed. We were fortunate to have an entire row together on an airplane where few others did. I felt especially grateful that there was an empty seat between us. We introduced ourselves, and when Donna heard my name, she replied, "That's my daughter's name. You are an angel."

On the contrary, I felt like I was so much less. I sat paralyzed in fear as Donna reached for my hands. When she stretched out her forearms toward me, she revealed several long, jagged scars. I looked up at her face and saw that her eyes brimmed with tears. She clutched my hands in hers and cried loud enough for surrounding passengers to hear, "I should've been the one! It should've been me!"

Terrified, I began to cry too.

"These scars on my arms are from bone cancer surgeries," she said, pointing to them. "He was the one who scraped people off the road. He was a paramedic." Donna explained that her husband had been hit by a drunk driver while on vacation. I knew that if I had been a stronger Christian, I could've reached out to her and led a prayer. Instead, I remained paralyzed.

"Do you have someone special in your life?" Donna asked.

"No," I replied.

"When you do," she said, "cherish every moment with him, because you never know when he'll be gone." I knew that God was speaking to me and that I would forever remember these words. But my reception was shrouded in a conviction that I was unprepared to embrace this grieving woman and in fear that this truth had been exposed to surrounding passengers.

After the airplane landed, I walked up the aisle behind Donna. I noticed that she staggered a bit. At that moment, I knew that although I could serve cocktails to passengers, I could not share Jesus with them.

Chapter 4

So we say with confidence, "The Lord is my helper; I will not be afraid. What can man do to me?"

—Hebrews 13:6

From the moment I met Jasmine, I saw Jesus. I knew that God had sent her to me as an example and to encourage me to overcome my fears. As I witnessed Jasmine's consistent demeanor of kindness throughout our trip, I decided that I wanted what she had. But I didn't know how to receive it. It wasn't the kindness that I wanted. It was the courage to be kind. I already had kindness secretly locked away in my heart, but I was too afraid to express it.

If God is love and love is kind and both God and love are powerful, then why did I feel so restrained from expressing kindness? Deep down, I knew it was because I feared that others would view my kindness as weakness, and I didn't want to be viewed as vulnerable at work.

God helped me to overcome this issue by Jasmine's witness that each time she operated in kindness to others, it was returned to her. He showed me that His kindness was disarming to people who expressed negative emotions because it touched their hearts. Simultaneously, He showed me that Jasmine, who allowed herself to be led by the Spirit, was also well-liked. This was important to me because I carried such fear of man in my soul. Through Jasmine, the Lord quelled my fear of persecution and rejection and released the courage in my heart to be kind.

Chapter 5

You, dear children, are from God and have overcome
them, because the one who is in you is greater than the
one who is in the world.

—1 John 4:4

I met Evan while working a trip in Pittsburgh. He was very
polite, well-groomed, and talented. During our trip, he
shared that he had an interest in the performing arts and
that, prior to flying, he had performed in traveling musi-
cals and on cruise ships as a dancer and singer. His back-
ground, linked with my interest in the visual arts, made
for lively conversation between us, and I learned much
from him. We agreed to get together on occasion to attend
a show or museum event.

About the same time I met Evan, I had begun writing for my airline's stewardess newsletter. I had an idea
to write a series of profiles on steward(esse)s, with Evan
being the first. My editor approved the idea, and I soon
interviewed and photographed Evan in his lovely home.

Although Evan seemed very respectful and apprecia-
tive of this opportunity at the time, soon after I had written the story, his demeanor changed drastically. In fact, he
asked me not to print the story, saying that he decided he
didn't want any attention focused on him. I didn't understand his change of heart, and I felt hurt and disappointed.
I hoped for more of an explanation, wondering whether I
had offended him in some way. But Evan remained very
reserved. I agreed to pull the story, and I sensed a distance
between us.

Months passed and I didn't see or hear from Evan. Then one day, as I flew to New York City to visit a friend, I noticed him seated several rows ahead of me. Beside him sat an elderly woman. Evan turned and saw me and invited me to meet his grandmother. I walked up to their row of seats and saw that in his grandmother's arms lay a large bouquet of red roses. Her face was exuberant. Evan explained that he was taking her to New York City and that it would be her first visit to the Big Apple. "She is queen for a day," he said.

"That's really sweet," I replied, still holding my hurt inside.

More months passed and no word from Evan. Then one day, a mutual stewardess friend of ours said to me that she had seen Evan in the crew lounge and that he looked to have lost a lot of weight. "Do you think he has AIDS?" she asked. This never occurred to me, and I felt shocked. By this time, Evan had moved out of the Pittsburgh area, and I didn't know how to contact him.

One day, I worked with a friend of Evan's. Through this friend, I learned some startling news: Evan had passed away. I understood Evan's official cause of death to be pneumonia. My heart sank with despair. I didn't get to say goodbye or pray over Evan. He was just gone. I felt so awful for harboring hurt. But God gave me a line of hope. Evan's friend gave me Evan's mother's address, where I could send condolences.

After our trip, I went home full of grief. In my tiny studio apartment, I cried out to God, asking Him for forgiveness and for what I could do. I pulled out the note that Evan's friend had given to me, and I looked at Evan's mother's name. It was Mary. Christmas was upon us, and I thought of Mary, Jesus' mother. What could I say to a mother who had just lost her son? To a friend's mother I had never met?

I pulled out a sheet of paper, and I began to write from my heart. I wept and I wept. It was one of the saddest letters I had ever written. I introduced myself to Mary and explained how I had come to know her son. Then I shared with her what Evan meant to me, how kind he was to me when I was new in Pittsburgh, how we used to attend the theater together, and how we laughed. Then I enclosed a copy of Evan's unpublished profile that I had written for the newsletter.

Days later, I received a heartfelt Christmas card from Mary, thanking me for befriending her son and for sending her my sentiments. She said that she would like to meet me sometime.

Up to now, I have not met Mary, but I still think of her. What remains with me is the memory of her son. I believe that God used Evan to convict me of unforgiving hurt and to help me understand more about the courage to face persecution. Evan was openly homosexual. He chose to live openly, knowing that many would not approve, knowing that he would face criticism and pain.

I realized that if Evan could find the courage to openly live a lifestyle that was unacceptable to many, who was I to not find courage in the Lord to live openly Christian? I knew that it was time for me to come out of the closet with Christianity. I knew that God was calling me to be bold for Him.

Chapter 6

"So do not fear, for I am with you; do not be dismayed, for I am your God. I will strengthen you and help you; I will uphold you with my righteous right hand."

—Isaiah 41:10

One day while working a flight, I noticed a mature woman seated at a window toward the rear of our Boeing 737-200. She seemed particularly fixated on an object outside, which I thought to be odd, given that we were traveling at a high speed and altitude. After a short while, I asked her what it was she saw. "Three rainbows," she replied. I scrambled across her body to see them, but by the time I reached the window, they were gone. The woman explained that each rainbow formed a circle, a parhelion. As she spoke, I felt a chill and a sense that these rainbows were a sign of something to come and that God would take care of me.

I informed the other two stewardesses about the rainbows. I was surprised to hear myself blurt out, "Something's going to happen, but we're going to be OK."

"I hope not!" the rookie stewardess replied. I wasn't sure whether the head stewardess took the message seriously, but she seemed as though she could handle any crisis with a great measure of leadership and grace.

The remainder of this particular flight was uneventful. I wasn't sure whether anyone except me thought anymore of the rainbows. As night fell, we flew another leg, landing in Baltimore. We boarded about forty-five passengers on what was to be our final leg for the night.

About ten minutes after takeoff, the captain rang the intercom. "Come up to the cockpit," he instructed. The new stewardess and I were already in the back galley. We looked at each other, then back up the aisle at the head stewardess, who looked back at us. All of us knew that this was not standard procedure for a normal flight. All of us knew that something was wrong. The head steward-ess immediately entered the flight deck and conferred with the captain. Within seconds, she exited and raced down the aisle toward us. "We have an emergency situation," she said. I felt my heart and my stomach fill with fear. She explained that the air starter valve light had illumi-nated in the flight deck and that the pilots had shut down the left engine to avoid a potential fire. She explained that we would circle back around to land in Baltimore. "Don't evacuate unless we hear from the cockpit," she said. "We have ten minutes to prepare the cabin."

That was the quickest ten minutes of my life! Adrena-line told me that we needed to get to the task at hand, but the Spirit told me that we should pray first. Up to this point, I had never prayed with coworkers. But we didn't have the luxury of time or circumstance for me to shrink back. So I fearfully blurted out to the girls, "I don't know about you two, but I'm going to pray!" To my surprise, the girls stood at the end of the aisle with me as I awkwardly led a short prayer: I reminded God of His promise, of the rainbows. And I asked Him to guide us in our tasks, to aid the pilots, and to keep us safe. After the prayer, the three of us quickly disbanded. The head stewardess announced to the passengers that we had a mechanical problem and that we were returning to Baltimore.

We prepared the cabin accordingly, picking up drink cups, checking seat belts, and dimming lights. As I walked through the dark cabin a final time, I made mental notes of where children and elderly people sat. I reaffirmed that there were no pets on board, and I searched for anyone else who might require special assistance in evacuating. I retrieved my emergency manual from my tote and then grabbed pillows and blankets, tossing them into the last row of seats just in case I needed to toss them outside to passengers. It was New Year's Eve, and snow covered the ground.

As I strapped into my shoulder harnesses in the rear of the aircraft, I felt isolated in the darkness. None of the passengers were seated toward the rear of the aircraft, and both the other stewardesses were seated up front. As I felt the plane descend, I began to pray. I confessed to God that I was frightened, despite His promise. Because of my fear, I felt that I had failed this test of faith and trust. I repeatedly asked Him to please take care of us. My mind kept drifting to potential circumstances: an engine fire, explosions, and burning metal searing my stockings to my legs. I managed to upset myself so much that I released my seat belt, stood up, and went for the fire extinguisher. I unbuckled the halon fire extinguisher with shaky fingers, brought it back to my jump seat, and clutched it like a shield. Again, I confessed my lack of trust to God, and then I asked Him to take care of my family. As we descended, the cabin was blanketed in silence except for one baby's muted cry that seemed to float in the air with us. Suddenly, I felt peace drift over me. From the serenity came a young woman's voice. A passenger had moved back a few rows, closer to me. I peered around the corner of the bulkhead and saw her sweet face. "Are we having an emergency?" she asked. I smiled and reassured her that everything would be OK.

As the plane continued to descend, the baby's cry continued to drift. Silence and peace prevailed. Soon, we hit the ground. Hard. I flinched, raising the fire extinguisher above my face, my finger on the pin, ready to pull it. Suddenly, I heard the copilot's cadence over the speaker: "Remain seated. Remain seated. Remain seated." So far, I hadn't seen any flames. There was no explosion. I peered around the bulkhead once more and saw passengers looking at each other in confusion. The ones on the left side of the aircraft stared out the windows. I released my shoulders and stood to look out the windows for fire. There was none. But there were emergency vehicles chasing our plane. I began to tear up as I witnessed so many people racing to help us. I felt grateful to God for sending support and for delivering us safely. As I thanked Him, I realized that through confronting my own mortality, God was able to break through a considerable measure of fear and pride in me and create space to put Him first.

Chapter 7

"I tell you, whoever acknowledges me before men, the
Son of Man will also acknowledge him before the angels
of God."

—Luke 12:8

I perceived Helen as gruff, based on her behavior during
the few times we had flown together. For this reason, I
felt uneasy about sharing my Christianity with her. Still, I
knew it was time to step out and witness. So after spending the first day of our trip getting reacquainted, I shared
that, after more than a decade, I had found a home church
and that I really liked it. "I needed to see the good side of
people," I said. "Do you go to church?" Helen confessed
that she did not, blaming her choice on legalism.

I replied that I was surprised at how much churches
had improved regarding this issue and that I had initially
stopped attending because I was afraid of being judged for
having been divorced.

I continued sharing my experiences about my new
church, how I saw people working together to raise funds
for an upcoming mission and how it moved me to tears. I
felt both surprised and encouraged that Helen listened so
intently. When I sensed that she was actually considering the notion of returning to church, I said, "Helen, if
they'll accept me after having done all the ungodly stuff
I've done, they'll accept anyone." Then I wrote down the
worship service information and handed it to her.

Within a few weeks, Helen called, saying that she
would meet me at my church. It was a joy to stand side

by side with her, singing and worshiping the Lord. After about a month, Helen enrolled her son in Sunday school. She later shared with me that her mother was relieved at this news. God grew my confidence as Helen and I continued to attend services.

Then along came Marcia, another stewardess, who had recently relocated to my area. Marcia had attended a Baptist church in North Carolina, where my family lived. This common ground encouraged me to invite Marcia to join Helen and me.

Soon, Marcia showed up at our church with her mother one Sunday. And she, too, enrolled her little boy in Sunday school. Helen and Marcia's presence was comforting to me and an answer to prayer because, being in a new church, I didn't know anyone there. And I had asked God to send me women who would join me. His choice of Helen, someone who I thought of as so unlikely, was evidence that God's ways are so much higher and that His mercy and grace are unending.

Each Sunday, I marveled at how God would use even me, someone who lacked in so many ways, to help these women and their children. Sharing the gospel in my workplace proved to me that I had nothing to fear; that if I did my part by stepping out in faith, God would, indeed, take care of the rest. His hand was surely upon us, because not once did Helen ridicule me. In fact, I saw her heart melt right before the Lord.

Chapter 8

"I have given you authority to trample on snakes and scorpions and to overcome all the power of the enemy; nothing will harm you."

—Luke 10:19

When Marge pulled out a Christian woman's magazine on the first day of our trip, I felt delighted. We each shared other Christian resources that we carried in our totes, including her spiritual warfare prayer. "You can make a copy of it," she said as she handed it to me. The prayer was just what I needed.

Anna, the other stewardess, walked to the back of the airplane and joined us. Marge and Anna discovered that they had once attended the same church. I knew that God's presence was strong and that He had purposed us to fly together.

Later in the flight, I had an opportunity to speak with Anna alone on our jump seat. It was then she shared that the Holy Spirit had given her the gift of prophecy and that she was an ordained prophetic prayer counselor.

As Anna and I shared our lives and God's Word, God enabled us to build trust in one another.

By the end of our second day of flying and sharing, Anna received an important word from the Holy Spirit about me. She said that the word was "critical." She then invited me to her room on our layover for a counseling session. I was curious, and I felt excited about what God had for me.

We arrived in Chicago at 11 a.m. Central Time. Anna and I agreed that I would visit her at 5 p.m. To prepare for the session, Anna suggested that I pray, confess my sins, and ask the Holy Spirit to reveal anything in particular that would hinder my reception of God's message to me. I did this as I knelt alongside my bed, and I asked Him to make me an open vessel to receive all that He had for me.

Within seconds, the Holy Spirit revealed to my conscious mind a particular unknown sin that I had been carrying for decades: pride. More specifically, He revealed that I felt embarrassed when people spoke in tongues. He then showed me the root of the sin: that I associated speaking in tongues with uneducated, unsophisticated people. Then He revealed that the ignorance that I saw in others was actually within myself. He revealed that I was deceived by Satan and that I was afraid of the power of speaking in tongues. This new awareness immediately humbled me. I confessed and asked God to help me fully understand His perspective on this issue. As I continued to pray, I felt at peace, and I was ready for the evening's session.

At 5 p.m., I knocked on Anna's door. She greeted me with a warm hug. As I pulled up a chair, I noticed several sheets of notes Anna had written. She glanced down at them and back at me. Her voice was soft and loving as she explained that she had spent time in prayer preparing for this session and that she had asked God to show her which issues He wanted her to address. Her notes were His list. Anna explained that God wanted to take me to higher ground, that I was at the crossroads, and that the choice was mine. I assured her that I was ready to do what God wanted me to do. Anna then led a long prayer. Then she had me pray alone and ask the Holy Spirit to reveal whatever He chose during this session.

Anna then handed me the long list of issues. It included sins that I had committed over my lifetime, many of which I was unaware. Also on the list were various types of curses. As I read this list, I was shocked, and I realized that God had opened my eyes to the evil that had been secretly operating in my life for a long time. Anna explained that these issues had created distance between Him and me and prevented me from receiving and giving all that He had for me. Up to this point, I had never thought of these items as sins, only as childish, harmless endeavors. Once again, I realized that I was deceived by Satan and that I had been a carnal Christian my entire life.

I chose to overcome this evil and get freedom. So, one by one, I confessed all of the sins on the list. Then Anna led me in a curse-breaking prayer. She prayed for me, both in and out of tongues. And this time I could enjoy hearing God's language spoken because I was free from so many heavy chains. Anna informed me that God wanted to give me the gift of tongues as well as the gift of prophecy. I gasped at God's expression of mercy and love for me. "Pray with me, Margaret," she said. "Put your hands up to mine." I placed my hands up against Anna's, and she said a prayer through which God imparted these gifts to me. Anna began speaking in tongues and then asked me to do the same. As I uttered a few soft-spoken words, I was awestruck at what God had done.

Anna then took my hands and led another long prophetic prayer in which she spoke to me the visions that God showed her. Her speech grew faster with each revelation, and she could hardly catch her breath between them.

At the end of our six-hour session, I asked her what the next step for me was, and she replied that I should just rest in the Lord. As I walked to my room, I felt like a new person, much lighter, joyful. I wanted to shout to the world what had just happened, that my soul had been set free.

The next day, after we returned to Philadelphia, Anna and I ate lunch together and discussed what God had done. As we walked to the gate to catch our next flight, she turned to me and asked me to be her friend. "I don't have any girlfriends," she said. "I've had trouble with women deceiving me in the past." Anna's words humbled my heart so deeply, not only because she was an instrument of God, full of wisdom and compassion, but also because she wanted to be my friend, like Jesus. God had blessed me with an answer to a lifelong prayer: a big sister. And to this day, we remain best friends.

Chapter 9

"Do you not say, 'Four months more and then the harvest'? I tell you, open your eyes and look at the fields! They are ripe for harvest."

—John 4:35

After returning to work, fresh from the mission fields of Havana, I was full of exuberance. I relentlessly shared the virtues of this mission with Kiko, a stewardess with whom I worked the coach cabin. Cuba was my first mission ever, and I still hadn't come down from the "high" of this life-changing experience.

Kiko was very kind and patient. She listened to each anecdote, each miracle, and there were many. In between them, Kiko was able to share a bit of her own testimony. She was Japanese and immigrated to America when she was a college student. While in college, she met a man, whom she married, and they settled in Maryland. Kiko's heart was hungry to return to her native Japan as a missionary. She and her husband prayed about their desire, seeking God's will. Kiko said that God ultimately closed the door to return to Japan, but He opened a door for ministry near her home. Kiko and her husband were obedient to God's calling. They decided to disciple a group of women in a local Korean community. Kiko explained a little about their ministry and her hospitality gift, how she hosted tea parties and Bible studies for the women, how she and her husband prayed that more people in the community would come to know the Lord.

As I continued to share the daily miracles involving the Cuba mission, Kiko asked a question that proved to be a revelation for me: "Don't you think miracles happen here in our own lives everyday?"

I didn't know why, but I knew I had just been convicted. "No," I said, not because I didn't believe God could perform them, but because I wasn't aware that I had ever seen a daily miracle.

As Kiko spoke about her and her husband's ministry, I could see her deep longing to be back in Japan. I listened more intently as she detailed the small miracles she experienced in their ministry, right in their own backyard. She then went to her suitcase and retrieved a workbook that she had been completing in a Bible study: *Experiencing God*. She shared it with me and suggested that I buy the book and immerse myself in it.

I bought *Experiencing God*, and I prayed that God would enable me to see His daily miracles all around me. Soon, He opened my eyes to see my flights as containerized mission fields, and I began to see miracles. I marveled and rejoiced in the Lord, praising Him for His power and intervention and for loving me enough to want to share His miracles with me. My job was never again the same. God had changed my perspective. What I viewed as a labor job was now a miraculous labor of love with so much meaning. I began to purposefully seek daily miracles that could potentially go unnoticed amid daily noise. My heart soared; I felt overjoyed that I didn't have to leave God's miracles back in Havana. And He used Kiko to accomplish this mission.

Chapter 10

As the body without the spirit is dead, so faith without
deeds is dead.

—James 2:26

Early in our trip, I found Jackie crying in the rear galley.
When I asked her what was the matter, she explained
that she frequently sat in her basement apartment drinking alcohol and that the man she had been seeing was married.

Jackie was in her early twenties and was new on the
job. I understood how wretched surviving the first five
years as a stewardess could be in coping with loneliness
and low pay.

I hugged Jackie, and I knew that the Holy Spirit used
her to move my heart into action. For years, I had been
considering writing an outreach newsletter for new stewardesses, but I had done nothing to bring it to fruition.

I thanked Jackie for sharing her story with me. Then
I asked her if she would like to help me with newsletter
ideas. Her eyes brightened.

When I returned home alone, I sat and looked over
our notes. I realized that by printing this newsletter, which
would include inexpensive local activities, a church direc-
tory, and prayer-line telephone numbers, I would be stepping out with my faith even more in my workplace.

As I produced the first issue, I was attacked with the
flu. It was clear to me that Satan didn't want this newsletter circulated. Nonetheless, I pressed on and prayed every
step of the way.

After making several hundred copies of this first issue, I knew I couldn't afford to keep it up each quarter. A union representative learned of the newsletter plans and informed me that she didn't think our employer would fund the venture. So I prayed for funding. And then I submitted the prototype to my crew base manager.

Soon after, I received a telephone call from her saying that she loved the newsletter and she would see that future issues were printed in-house. The airline agreed to pay for it completely. I felt overjoyed. God provided, and I was on a roll.

When I sat down to work on the next issue, my computer crashed. Entirely. Several hundreds of dollars later, it was repaired. But now I was behind deadline. So I prayed for God to send me others who would help, and He did. People began to contribute ideas and to stuff the stewardess's mailboxes.

Soon, stewardesses left notes in my mailbox and sent e-mails thanking me. I watched as they read copies of the newsletter in the crew lounge and on our trips. I felt so blessed and hopeful that it would help to change their lives for the better.

During the next three issues, I was afflicted with pneumonia, another computer crash, and an intestinal issue that drained most of my energy for months. Even so, I pressed on and continued to pray for protection.

Soon after, I felt exhausted and my joy in this project began to wane. Finally, one day I threw up my hands in haste and proclaimed to God, "I need help! What do You want me to learn from this!?" Then I heard God's still, small voice reply, "Just waiting for you to ask."

Chapter II

In all your ways acknowledge him, and he will make your paths straight.

—Proverbs 3:6

One evening, our crew was informed that only five passengers were booked on our flight. I was the head stewardess, and, as an unexpected blessing to the passengers, I asked the customer agent to seat all of them in first class. He agreed and then proceeded up the loading bridge to commence boarding.

I greeted each passenger as they entered our airplane, and I felt stunned as they each passed by me with an attitude, without acknowledging me. As they took their newly upgraded seats, one of them said, "The agent said we could sit here."

After takeoff, they spoke to me as though I was their slave, telling me what to bring them. I walked into the galley, my pride hurt and my love walk tested. "If they only knew that I was the one who invited them to sit up here," I thought. "They haven't a clue."

Suddenly, the Holy Spirit enlightened me: "This is how I feel when you don't acknowledge Me for all that I provide for you."

This conviction grabbed hold of my heart in a way that I shall never forget. I repented and thanked God for this revelation. I then thanked Him for what I had been taking for granted at work for years, for even having a job and for safe flights.

Chapter 12

Jabez cried out to the God of Israel, "Oh, that you would bless me and enlarge my territory! Let your hand be with me, and keep me from harm so that I will be free from pain." And God granted his request.

—1 Chronicles 4:10

God used the book, *The Prayer of Jabez*, to give me understanding and to open my eyes to the abundant opportunities for service at work. After reading this treasure of a book, I prayed each week for God to choose trips for me and to give me divine appointments.

On one particular trip, I had a layover in Jacksonville, Florida. I walked down to the hotel restaurant the following morning to find that most of the tables were already filled with what resembled a convention of people. In my search for a seat, God steered me toward a particular table where a mature couple sat. I smiled and asked to join them.

I learned that this couple was in town to attend a Baptist convention and that Pastor Carl was, in fact, head of a congregation in upstate New York. His wife, Joanne, and I discussed travel and books and church.

Soon, my captain and copilot spotted me and joined us at the table. We listened to Pastor Carl share about his new wood-burning furnace that heated his church and outbuildings. I felt so blessed to have met this lovely couple in such a surprising way.

After breakfast, I went up to my room and prayed. I had felt a strong connection with Joanne, and I asked God to give me another opportunity to meet with her. Then I packed my suitcase and headed out the door.

When I reached the lobby, behold, there was Joanne and Pastor Carl. "I'm so glad I got to see you again," I said.

"Me too," Joanne replied. "I prayed after I saw you, and I asked God to give me another opportunity to speak to you."

"Me too!"

With this, Joanne gave me a flyer about her church and a gospel newsletter. She also handed me a tract, asking me to give it to someone who needed it. When I looked at the tract, I saw that a picture of pennies was printed on the top margin of the front page. I shared with Joanne that I had found several pennies the day before and that God frequently used pennies as signs of encouragement while on my mission to Cuba. Joanne seemed delighted, and we agreed to keep in touch.

My crew and I flew to Philadelphia and then prepared to board our next flight to Boston. I listened as I heard the first passenger walk down the loading bridge. "Come on," the woman instructed her young son repeatedly. I walked out onto the bridge to see if I could help. The woman carried a car seat and a shopping bag while her two-year-old son toddled slowly toward her. "May I help?" I asked.

"I've got it," she replied. When her son reached the threshold of the airplane, I reached down and picked him up and brought him into the plane. I was concerned that his toes would get caught in the seam between the bridge and the aircraft threshold. His mother thanked me as they headed to their seats.

After takeoff, another stewardess, Tara, tended to the woman, helping her find a spot to change her son's diaper. I noticed that Tara was very kind to any request the woman asked of her, and there were many. I was impressed with Tara's patience.

After we cleared the cabin for landing, Tara walked up to the jump seat and sat next to me. Her face appeared a little distressed. "That woman's husband just died," she said.

When the woman deplaned in Boston, my crew and I did also. We were scheduled to sit in Boston for a few hours before returning to Philadelphia for our final flight. I quickly separated myself from the crew and walked up the concourse to find the woman. En route, I prayed that God would give me His courage and wisdom to witness to this woman.

I stepped up to her and shared with her that Tara had informed me about her late husband, and I offered my condolences. "I have something to give you," I said. "Someone special gave this to me this morning and asked me to give it to someone who needed it. I think that someone may be you." I explained that the tract was from a pastor's wife and that I had prayed for God to show me who needed it most. "Jesus loves you," I said.

The woman accepted the tract gingerly, as if no one had ever given her a gift before. "Oh, thank you," she said sweetly. The woman then explained that her husband had been very sick for nine months with brain cancer. She also shared that his family didn't like her but that they wanted to keep her young son and raise him in Puerto Rico. She went on to say that she had no choice but to bury her late husband in Puerto Rico because his family provided the money for his funeral, money she didn't have. "It's not so bad for me," she said. "But for him," she added, pointing to her young son.

God melted my heart and enabled me to feel such mercy and compassion for this woman. I could barely hold back my tears. I told her that I would like to pray for her and her son, that Jesus would send kind people to help her and to befriend her. She thanked me again, then picked up her son and went down the escalator.

I still had a couple of hours to pass before boarding my final flight for the evening. So I found a quiet corner near an unoccupied gate, and I sat and prayed.

Later, when I boarded the flight back to Philadelphia, I shared the news with Tara. After we took off, Tara got serious and turned to me on the jump seat. "I'm Catholic," she said, "and I haven't gone to church in a long time. God gets mad at me for that."

"Oh no," I replied. "He just waits for us to come back to Him. Besides, how can He be mad at you? He just used you to extend His patience and loving-kindness to that woman."

Tara smiled.

The next day, I wrote Joanne a letter about the woman whom God chose to receive the tract.

Weeks later, after Joanne and Pastor Carl returned from their journey, I received a card from her saying that she was delighted to hear the news and that she had commissioned a ladies prayer group in her church to pray for the young widow and her young son. I felt awed at what God had done.

Chapter 13

"And I myself will be a wall of fire around it," declares the Lord, "and I will be its glory within."

—Zechariah 2:5

After working my first flight to Orlando one day, I bought a tuna sandwich and sat near a window, just outside the airport concourse. About halfway through my lunch, a mature woman and her husband walked up and asked whether anyone was sitting across from me. I invited them to join me. The woman's husband pulled out a book and read while she struck up a conversation with me. Barbara was her name.

As Barbara and I talked, I began to detect that she was a Christian. I felt compelled to tap into her spiritual wisdom. I mentioned to Barbara that each time I worked on the outreach newsletter, Satan attacked me. I shared with her that I had prayed for protection, but the attacks continued.

Barbara began coughing. "Satan is attacking me now," she said, in between coughs. "He doesn't want me to tell you this." Barbara informed me that I needed to pray the shed blood of Christ, that if I beseeched God through Christ's sacrificial blood, Satan would have no influence over me. Then Barbara proceeded to pray for me. She asked God for Christ's blood to pour over me and for His "firewall" protection.

No one had ever shared this with me before, especially a passenger in the middle of an airport. But this was the second day in a row that a Christian had mentioned the shed blood of Jesus to me.

Barbara assured me that God was giving me a tool with which to pray. I had been praying for God to lead me to sources to teach me what else I needed to do to receive His protection, and God used Barbara to deliver His word and to continue to intercede for me.

Chapter 14

... For the Lord your God will bless you in all your harvest and in all the work of your hands, and your joy will be complete.

—Deuteronomy 16:15

Jerry Goldstein, along with his wife, Sarah, had just returned from Greece one day. Their trip was a fiftieth wedding anniversary gift from their three children. After deplaning, Jerry collapsed at Sarah's feet. "My husband has a heart condition!" Sarah shouted.

At that moment, Jan, a stewardess from my airline, happened to walk by. With her was a passenger whom she was escorting to a customer service counter. Alarmed, Jan immediately ran to retrieve an automatic electronic defibrillator (AED), which had been placed in the Baltimore Washington International airport just weeks earlier.

In the meantime, the passenger tended to Jerry, who lay unconscious. The passenger, who happened to be a medical student at Johns Hopkins University, began CPR. A security guard heard the commotion and handed Jan an AED. Jan raced back to Jerry's still body, connected the electrodes to his chest, and administered one shock.

With this, Jerry regained consciousness. The paramedics soon arrived and rushed Jerry to St. Agnes Hospital in Baltimore. In the emergency room, Sarah watched while cardiologists worked on her husband. This was Jerry's third heart-related emergency, and his own cardiologist was at Mt. Sinai Hospital.

A press conference, which featured a reunion between Jerry, Sarah, and Jan, was held a few months later at the airport. "She's our angel," Sarah said of Jan as the media cameras flashed. Looking at Jerry's smiling face, there were no signs that he had just survived heart arrhythmia.

This story sparked my heart. The editor of my airline's newsletter had assigned it to me. And I wanted to be sure that I honored God by including Him in this story that would be circulated to stewardesses system wide. So I asked Sarah how this incident changed her.

She shared that when she was in the emergency room with Jerry, a nun walked in and asked her if she wanted to pray. When Sarah revealed that she and Jerry were Jewish, the nun reminded her that everyone is God's creation. "It makes me believe that there is only one God," Sarah said. "It was as if He was saying, 'I'm going to put you through this, but I'm going to take care of you.'"

As I included these spiritual nuggets in the story, I knew that my heart for writing was God's. He had rewarded my faithfulness by giving me a breakthrough of increase in territory and favor. And now the entire stewardess department would read about Him and His miracles.

Chapter 15

You are the God who performs miracles; you display
your power among the peoples.

—Psalm 77:14

When I first met Sue, I noticed the tiny diamond cross
pendant around her neck. I had prayed that God
would choose every crew member on our trip, and I believed that He chose Sue.

As soon as we stepped onto the aircraft and stowed
our luggage, Sue explained how she had received her trip.
She said that crew scheduling had assigned this trip to her
after they erroneously passed by her name on the seniority
list. Any stewardess who has ever dealt with these circumstances would likely know that such a treasure of a trip
with a long Aruba layover wouldn't have still been available without a miracle from God. What's more, Sue was
based in a different city than the rest of us.

While Sue continued to share her amazing circumstances with another stewardess, I walked into the lavatory and prayed over our airplane and crew and passengers. Afterwards, I placed crosses over the inside of each
door and one large cross on the outside of the passenger
entrance door with anointing oil.

When I finished, I approached Sue and pulled her from
the first-class cabin into coach so that I could speak with
her privately. "I see that you're Christian," I said, pointing
to the cross around her neck.

"Yes," Sue replied. "It's 'higher' than my rings." Sue explained that her husband had given her the diamond cross

necklace and that she had requested it because she wanted a symbol of Jesus to hang higher than her wedding rings.

I took Sue's hand in mine. "I have something to share with you," I said. Then I explained how I pray before each trip for God to choose a trip for me and to choose every crew member. "He chose you to be on this trip," I said. "You're supposed to be here."

Sue's eyes filled with tears. She looked up, lifted her palms, and said, "Praise the Lord!" Then she turned to me, and, with a big smile, she said, "I knew when I got this trip that it was from God, and I thanked Him." Sue and I embraced.

As we became busy with passengers, I excitedly asked God to reveal His purpose for this divine appointment. During a break, I walked into the flight deck to see if the pilots wanted drinks. When I stepped in, I looked down to find a dime on the floor behind the captain's seat. I knew in my spirit that it was a sign from God, as He had frequently given me coins. I knew that this captain was special to God's heart. And I believed that God wanted me to pray for him because, earlier that morning, he had shared that he was divorced and that his son was mildly autistic. He also shared that one of his parents had died five months earlier and that a colleague had been recently diagnosed with liver cancer.

I stepped out of the flight deck and walked down the aisle to the rear galley. There I found Sue talking to Tamara, another stewardess. Tamara looked up at me with a smile. "God speaks to Sue," she said. "And she writes down what He says." I marveled at how God was at work on that airplane.

Later in the flight, Sue walked up front and joined me on the jump seat. She shared that God was in the process of preparing her for a healing ministry and that she had taken a year's worth of workshops on healing at her church. I expressed my interest in this gift of healing, and Sue referred me to several books on the topic.

She and I agreed that we needed to pray. So after landing in Charlotte, we walked past security, and Sue led me into the airport chapel. In all the years I had been flying, I had never noticed that chapel. Once inside, we thanked God for bringing us together, and we asked for His firewall of protection to surround Sue. We prayed for the captain. Then we asked God to open doors of healing opportunities for us and to continue to link us together.

The next morning, while on a layover, I checked my e-mail. As I read an e-mail from a religious service to which I subscribe, I noticed that there was a link to Sue's church. I knew that God had used Sue to plant a seed concerning the healing ministry, and now the very training tapes that she had studied were suddenly available to me.

About two months later, I crossed paths with Sue again on a loading bridge while switching aircraft.

Then about a year later, God brought Sue and me together on another airplane. Sue shared that Rev. Cal Pierce was scheduled to speak on the topic of healing at a local church near her home in Charlotte. I expressed that I would like to attend, and she invited me to fly down and stay with her and her husband during this conference.

The first day of the healing conference was scheduled on my day off. I spent the night in Sue's home and then flew back the next day to prepare to work a trip. After seeking the Lord for His help with logistics, He blessed me with the only trip that had two Charlotte layovers, one on the final evening of the conference. I was able to purchase tapes that filled me in on the second evening that I missed. More importantly, during the last night of this conference, I received an impartation of healing anointing that would open my eyes to even more of God's miraculous wonders.

Chapter **16**

Praise be to the God and Father of our Lord Jesus Christ,
the Father of compassion and the God of all comfort,
who comforts us in all our troubles, so that we can comfort those in any trouble with the comfort we ourselves
have received from God.

—2 Corinthians 1:3-4

The first time Donna and I flew together, we encoun-
tered a medical emergency. A man passed out in the
rear galley and hit his head on the metal bulkhead trim,
cutting his ear. Donna caught him before he landed on the
galley floor. By the time I got to the rear of the aircraft, the
man had regained consciousness and was sitting upright in
a passenger seat. Donna's arms and hands were so covered
in this man's blood that I thought she was bleeding too.

We called MedLink, an emergency consultation service, for help. Thankfully, two nurses were on board the
aircraft and offered assistance. We learned that the man had
a pacemaker, a feeding tube, and a host of serious medical
conditions. We weren't sure whether the man would make
it, and we were too close to our destination city to divert
to another airport but far enough away that the minutes
seemed like hours. So during the remainder of our flight,
Donna and I prayed on the edges of our seats.

At the end of our flight, paramedics placed the man
on a stretcher. He pleaded not to be taken to a hospital
because he knew that he would have to be admitted for a
while. Jesus filled my heart with compassion for this man,

and I stood crying and praying for him as he was wheeled away.

The second time Donna and I flew together was September 10, 2001. We began our two-day trip in Baltimore, flew to Florida, then up to Dulles International airport. Our crew was booked to stay over in Virginia. Everyone except me, that is. I had a vacation day scheduled for the following day, Tuesday, September 11, 2001. It was a day that I had tried months earlier, in vain, to reschedule because it was a straggler. Clearly, God had a specific purpose for me to be off that day. On the afternoon of the tenth, I bid Donna and the crew goodbye at Dulles, and I drove home.

Donna and the crew returned to Dulles the following morning of September 11, 2001 and took off for Orlando. While in flight, the pilots received the shocking news about the World Trade Center bombings, and they were ordered to land immediately. By then, the closest airport happened to be their scheduled destination. And so they landed in Orlando, where they remained for the next five days.

As I sat alone in my condo the evening of the bombings, I felt the Holy Spirit escalate His peace in me. I didn't understand this at first because I felt the Holy Spirit's profound presence in a new way, and it was certainly not how I had felt on previous occasions when airplanes had crashed. I can only attempt to describe it as peace and joy unspeakable, beyond what my emotions would allow. I couldn't even feel guilty about feeling lifted because the Spirit's power was so much greater than my own. I knew that God had a purpose for doing this, and I believe that He escalated me above emotional anguish so that I could continue to fly and help others. I would need His strong presence. It would be the only way.

As soon as I could get a telephone call through, I spoke with Donna on her cell phone. She seemed a little shaken as she gave me her report of what happened. She expressed that she was concerned about her nineteen-year-old son who was home alone on the other side of Baltimore City from me. I promised her that I would check on him. And then we prayed.

When Donna and the crew made it home, she told me how, during their ordeal, crew scheduling was overwhelmed, how they had instructed the crew to go to the airport a few times, only to find that there wasn't an airplane to fly back to their base. Each time, they returned to the Orlando hotel. Finally, on their last attempt, the other stewardess in the crew broke down and cried in the terminal. She had a two-year-old son at home whom she missed very much. She was also scheduled to settle on a house during this captive period. We prayed again.

I realized that this situation was my first mission in helping people who were affected by the September 11 crisis.

Chapter 17

God is our refuge and strength, an ever-present help in trouble.

—Psalm 46:1

On my first trip after September 11, 2001, I knew I would be facing new territory. One week after the bombings, God gave me a trip with a New York City layover. I praised the Lord and asked Him to protect us and guide my every step. I felt the Spirit's strength abound within me, and I knew I was ready, like a soldier.

In between one of our flights, I sat in a passenger seat, reading *Left Behind*. Tess, the head stewardess, approached me and asked, "How can you read that at a time like this?"

I smiled and replied, "How can I not?" I explained to Tess that I was a Christian and that I had prayed for God's peace and protection over us and our airplane. Tess thanked me for my wisdom and then explained that she had begun to attend church with her brother and that he had encouraged her to develop a deeper personal relationship with the Lord.

After takeoff, Jo, the stewardess who worked the coach cabin with me, walked to the rear jump seat and sat down next to me. She lamented that a couple of men who were seated up front stared at her and Tess during takeoff. Jo was clearly scared. I stood up and walked to the front of the airplane to look at the men's eyes. On my walk up, I prayed that the Holy Spirit would give me clear discernment as to their character. When I reached the front, I turned around and walked back down the aisle and glanced at the men.

I returned to the back of the airplane and informed Jo that I wanted to pray about these circumstances, these men. I asked her whether she wanted to join me. Jo declined, saying that she wasn't religious and that she wasn't sure about any specific higher power. I excused myself and locked myself in the lavatory and prayed once again for protection and peace and for the presence of angels.

After Jo and I served the passengers, we nestled into a row of seats to ourselves. She pulled out her camera and clicked away at the views outside her window. "I like sunsets," she said. "I have lots of pictures of them." While Jo continued to snap shots of God's graceful beauty, she shared a little about herself. I learned that she had been a professional firefighter prior to becoming a stewardess. "Tess was a firefighter too," she said. "Volunteer."

On the next day of our trip, we boarded a flight in Orlando, bound for New York LaGuardia. As the airplane filled with passengers, a man walked to the back and approached me. "Have you noticed there are some Arab men on the plane?" he asked.

"No," I replied, not having walked through the cabin yet.

"Aren't you concerned?" he said, nervously.

"No."

"Well, I am," the man retorted, "and so is my wife." The man said that he would like to deplane and take a later flight. I invited him to do so, adding that people of Arab descent may be on his next flight and that there may not be any seats available. He quickly discussed the issue with his wife, and they decided to deplane. I spoke another affirmation of protection for us and over them as they exited.

Our airplane arrived in New York safely. As we passed near the island of Manhattan, we gazed out the windows to see the smoldering mass that was once the World Trade Towers. My heart sank.

Later, the ride in the hotel van into Manhattan was somber. I had made plans to meet my longtime friend, Ellen, that evening for dinner. Ellen had lived in New York City for a couple of decades. She knew the city well. She explained to me that everyone she knew had known someone who had died in the bombings.

That evening, she and I headed out to one of her favorite restaurants in her neighborhood. Along the way, we passed the city morgue and the trailers that were used to haul human remains from the bombing site. We also passed Belleview Hospital, observing the many makeshift memorials that lined its long entrance.

As we sat at a swank restaurant eating our gourmet food, I realized that I had never witnessed the gospel to Ellen. So I asked her, "Do you have a Bible?" Ellen hesitated and then said, "No." I knew that she had been raised Catholic and had grown away from the church, but I never knew whether she had a personal relationship with Jesus Christ. Through our restaurant window, I saw a large bookstore across the street. As soon as we finished our meals, I took Ellen's hand and led her across the street. "I'm buying you your first Bible," I said.

I tore the plastic off the Bible and turned to Jeremiah 29:11-13, which I chose because Ellen had recently experienced a divorce. Once back at Ellen's apartment, I read the scripture to her and handed the open Bible to her. I shared how God had a plan for her life and what having a personal relationship with Jesus meant. I advised her to attend church and to seek salvation.

The next day, Tess and Jo seemed more frightened. Tess's fears surfaced in what appeared to be conviction and humility. Jo's concerns surfaced in edginess and irritability. I learned that both of these women stayed in their rooms during most of the layover. I have no doubt that having been firefighters, they were even more aware than I of the raw nature of the destruction that lay just blocks south of our comfortable hotel.

As the day progressed, God presented more opportunities to share Jesus with these women. Tess was very receptive. Jo, on the other hand, became angry to the point of mild tantrums. Still, Tess thanked me for my wisdom, right in front of Jo. I knew God was encouraging me through Tess. And I acknowledged that the wisdom I exhibited was not my own.

In the end, Jo apologized for what she described as her "drama." I knew that the Holy Spirit had convicted her and kept me steadfast. Through these experiences, the Spirit illuminated to me that the post-September 11 trips, which He assigned to me, offered greater opportunities for outreach, prayer, and protection.

Chapter 18

Do not be anxious about anything, but in everything, by prayer and petition, with thanksgiving, present your requests to God.

—Philippians 4:6

On October 11, 2001, exactly one month after the bombings, I sat in a passenger seat on a Boeing 737, with the rest of my crew nearby. We were parked at a gate in Baltimore, about to begin our one-day trip. I peered out the window and spotted a coworker on the ramp. Ian and I had worked together during my college days, heaving bags in and out of cargo bins. Since then, our paths crossed occasionally on a loading bridge or on a flight.

On this day, Ian was perched atop a bag-loader, waiting for his plane to come in on the next gate. The sun beamed down on his face as he stared straight ahead in contemplation. After a moment, he lowered his head and placed his face in his hands. I wasn't sure whether he was just tired or whether there was a problem, but I sensed that I should go down there.

As I descended the loading bridge stairs, one of Ian's comrades saw me and yelled out, "Are you going to help Ian pray?" I thought he was joking. Ian heard our exchange and took his face out of his hands and looked up at me. A smile spread across his face at the sight of his longtime acquaintance, and he leaped off the belt loader.

"Are you really praying?" I asked.

"Yeah."

I couldn't miss the look of desperation and sadness in his eyes. "What's up?"

Ian threw up his hands as he often did in his expressions of frustration. He released a torrent of worries that had gushed into his life as a result of the bombings and the economic downturn. He explained that due to drastic cuts in our airline's flight schedule, he had not been able to secure overtime hours, upon which he and his wife and their three children depended. "My paycheck has been cut in half," he said. Ian elaborated a little more before venting the most worrisome effects: He could no longer afford to keep his eight-year-old daughter in Christian school. And she could not concentrate in class because she was so concerned about her father's safety. "She has nightmares," he said.

I knew I didn't have much longer to chat with Ian, as passenger boarding time was near. And I knew that God had sent me down to Ian to pray for him and his family. I promised Ian that I would pray for his needs to be met and for comfort and peace for his daughter. We said goodbye as Ian's flight arrived at the gate next door. I dashed up the loading bridge stairway, feeling the warm sun on my face and thanking God for the opportunity to reach out to a friend and lift him up.

After returning home that evening, I attended my weekly Bible study. There, I shared Ian's story and asked for prayer for him, his daughter, and all airline workers and their families. An army of a dozen women prayed for them that night, and I had no doubt that God answered.

Chapter 19

Lord, I have heard of your fame; I stand in awe of your deeds, O Lord. Renew them in our day, in our time make them known; in wrath remember mercy.

—Habakkuk 3:2

As we flew over Manhattan one evening, I sat in a window seat on our Boeing 737 and observed the World Trade Center rubble under bright white lights. Although I had worked several previous flights into LaGuardia airport since the bombings, I had only seen the carnage from a daytime sky, which had been blurred with smoke and ash. This time, I saw what was once a tall, seemingly indestructible wall of one of the towers shoot up out of the rubble as a jagged shard, a tortured fragment. I felt sadness in my heart, and I prayed.

The next morning, I opted to ride on the earliest flight back to my crew base in Baltimore. I was assigned an aisle seat on the left side of the Dash 8 aircraft. During boarding, the working stewardess invited me to sit in the exit row on the right side. I thought nothing of it except as an opportunity to spread out and read my newspaper.

I switched seats, and I soon spotted a story about a man who, for years, searched to find his father, whom he hadn't seen since age eighteen. Sadly, the man's father died in the World Trade Center bombings. The son didn't know about his father's passing until he searched public records and discovered that his father had worked there. It was one of the most touching and sad stories that I had ever read.

The plane took off, and I pressed on reading the article. My eyes filled with tears, partly out of compassion for the son, partly for the pain and turmoil that his father endured throughout his life, and partly due to God's grace that He miraculously let my own father live after two battles with cancer. The further I read, the more humbled I felt. My heart poured out overwhelmingly to God. I prayed for Him to extend His comfort, peace, and healing to the son.

When I opened my eyes, I looked out the window and saw a parhelion. It was formed through a thin layer of clouds beneath our plane, just below the engine cowling. A shadow of our airplane was in the center of this beautiful circle. It looked like both a bulls-eye and a multicolored halo right over New York.

As we sped forward, the clouds and the parhelion dissipated. In the clearing, the scenery below turned from urban to country within a couple of blinks. Beautiful emerald green hills were crowned with clumps of autumn foliage, which soon turned into stripes of farmland before reaching Baltimore.

I believe that God burdened my heart to intercede for this son and for New York and that He demonstrated signs of His abounding mercy, grace, and love for them.

Chapter 20

"For I know the plans I have for you," declares the
Lord, "plans to prosper you and not to harm you, plans
to give you hope and a future."

—Jeremiah 29:11

After finishing a trip late one morning, I crossed paths
with a steward, David. I greeted him with a big smile
and a hug. David, however, seemed troubled. In fact, his
eyes almost immediately grew red and filled with tears.
I asked him what was the matter. "You don't know?" he
replied. "I've been furloughed."

This didn't surprise me because God had shown me
a vision of David's face earlier that morning, and I knew
that He wanted me to pray for him. It was several weeks
after the New York terrorist bombings, and we were seeing
manifestations of our airline's financial troubles.

I believe that God has a special heart for David, who
happens to be an Orthodox Jew. I had known him casually for about six years at this point. He used to be the sole
steward who worked many of my flights between LaGuardia and Baltimore when I commuted to graduate school.
During those times, David seemed sensitive and frequently
in need of compassion. I knew he felt endeared to me because he had once told me that I was the only stewardess
who had been kind to him on those flights. I knew the
truth: that the kindness he saw was that of Jesus.

"I should have stayed with the commuter," David said
to me on this late morning. "Eleven years for nothing."
David had resigned at the small aircraft division a year and

a half earlier when our airline hired him. I knew that Jesus wanted to reassure David through me. So I took David's hands in mine and said, "Everything is going to be all right." David suddenly looked away from me, his eyes growing redder. "Just pray, David. Trust God."

David pulled away from me and said hastily, "I did pray. I prayed that I wouldn't be furloughed, and God let it happen anyway."

"David, God loves you and wants what's best for you," I said. "Ask Him what He wants for you and trust Him. Maybe He has something better in mind."

"I have to go check in for my trip," he said, frustrated.

As David walked away, I shouted, "Jeremiah 29:11! Read it!"

David turned and pointed at me. "That's your end of the Bible!" he shouted, erroneously.

"No, it's our end!" This was the first time I had ever shouted scripture in an airport. It felt liberating. As I walked out to catch the parking van, I said another prayer for David, asking God to comfort and reassure him.

One week later, while in the midst of working a trip, I stood on a loading bridge in New York's LaGuardia airport. I waited for the crew to deplane so that I could board and work the departing flight. The first stewardess walked off, then the second. The third one, to my surprise, was David. Believing that there are no coincidences, I approached him exuberantly. "How are you?" I asked again.

"I'm taking the six-month voluntary leave," he replied.

Shortly after our initial conversation, our airline offered voluntary leaves of absence to all steward(esse)s. Approximately two thousand stewardesses opted to take the leaves, meaning that David moved up considerably on the seniority list and was ultimately spared an involuntary furlough. If he hadn't chosen to take the voluntary leave of absence, he would have remained flying. As it was, David decided he needed rest, so he chose the voluntary leave. This was a better deal than the involuntary furlough because David could return to the airline in six months as opposed to not knowing whether the airline would ever bring him back from an involuntary furlough.

"I'm so glad that God answered your prayer," I said.

The whole time God enabled me to encourage David, He reaffirmed my own faith, and He reinforced that I shouldn't necessarily accept the facts of a situation as His truth.

Chapter 21

No, in all these things we are more than conquerors through him who loved us.

—Romans 8:37

Three months after the September 11 bombings, I transferred to Philadelphia, due to my airline's downsizing and ultimate closure of my Baltimore crew base. Even the outreach newsletter that God had led me to write for Baltimore-based stewardesses came to a screeching halt due to lack of finances. After several years of having been based in Baltimore, I was uneasy about these changes, and I prayed for God to intervene and help me amid the uncertainty I felt.

I was relieved to see Dolly, also a former Baltimore stewardess, on my first trip in my new crew base. Thankfully, Dolly was familiar with our aircraft, and she flew the position in charge. I knew God had answered my prayers.

Well into our trip, Dolly stumbled in the galley and twisted her ankle. She sat on the galley floor, clearly in pain. "Are you all right?" I asked.

"Yeah," she replied, clutching her ankle. "I think so." I grabbed a trash bag from a compartment and filled it with ice. Then I handed it to her, along with a pillow.

As I sat on the jump seat and kept her company, Dolly opened up more about her personal life. She said that her daughter, Tiffany, was a challenge in her teen years. I asked Dolly whether she and Tiffany attended church. She replied that they attended a traditional church service, one that Tiffany didn't like. Dolly laughed and said that she and Tiffany didn't see eye to eye on many areas of Tiffany's life. As Dolly talked, the Holy Spirit spoke to me. He instructed me to pray over her ankle. "You've got to be kidding," I thought. "I can't do that. What will she think?"

As Dolly continued sharing, I felt distracted and increasingly fearful of praying out loud for Dolly's healing. Up to this point, I had not laid hands on someone for the purpose of physical healing. This single mom was clearly struggling physically as well as emotionally and financially. I felt compassion for her, but I froze in fear and couldn't act on the Holy Spirit's calling. I realized that I still hadn't fully overcome fear of man. It was as if seeing Dolly's familiar face threw me into my past.

Later, in my hotel room, I confessed my disobedience to God, and I prayed for Dolly and Tiffany and for me.

Several months later, I bumped into Dolly in the Philadelphia terminal. We greeted each other with a big hug. She said that she was delighted that Tiffany was attending a new church and was involved in a youth group. She also mentioned that she, herself, had just had a physical examination. She shared that she was now in her early forties and was diagnosed with high cholesterol and depression and that she had been taking antidepressants. Instead of praying for her right there in the airport, I assured her that I would pray for her later.

Afterwards, I realized that, throughout my transition, God was in control, and He had a purpose. He was expanding my territory by leading me to a larger crew base with more stewardesses and by leading me to operate in His gift of healing. He had tested my boldness to reveal the fear issue, which He would help me to overcome.

Chapter 22

May the Lord make your love increase and overflow for each other and for everyone else, just as ours does for you.

—1 Thessalonians 3:12

As I served first class on an Airbus 319, Sidney helped me. This was only my second time working this type of airplane, and I depended on her. Although Sidney answered all of my questions, she did so in a tone that was quick, as if she didn't want to be bothered. I was still uncomfortable with stewardesses I didn't know, and I knew to leave my anxiety at the altar. So as soon as I could, I went into the lavatory and prayed, asking God to help me love Sidney as He did.

When we arrived in Grand Cayman, most of the crew chose to deplane and stretch their legs. I hadn't worked any flights to the Caribbean islands since September 11, and I was concerned about increased security measures. I asked Sidney whether we needed to fill out a custom's form, to which she replied, "No."

"But the manual says we need one," I replied.

"Believe whatever you want," she said with an attitude. Then she darted off the airplane.

After a while, the crew returned to the aircraft. Sidney plopped into a first-class seat in front of me. The copilot, who sat across the aisle from me, politely asked me, "So, Margaret, how do you like Philly?"

"I like it just fine," I replied, "but I've noticed that I've been flying with some miserable people lately."

"Welcome to Philly!" he said laughing.

Suddenly, Sidney came over the back of the seat toward me. "I'll tell you why I'm so miserable!" she said, raising her voice. Then she offered a list of excuses for her misery: being a single mother, receiving no child support, working long hours, feeling forced to be based on the east coast when she'd rather be based on her native west coast, having a limited education and therefore few choices of career options. She finished by saying that she was stuck with no place to go.

In the midst of Sidney's lamentations, Jesus surprised me by filling my heart with His love for her. I actually felt a physical manifestation of this. "There's only one solution," I said. "Divine intervention."

Sidney calmed down a bit and replied that she had not been raised with any type of religion but that she and her five-year-old daughter had ventured to church last Easter and were later baptized. I realized that I was faced with a baby Christian. "Sidney," I said. "I have something to share with you." I explained to Sidney that I pray each week and ask God to choose a trip and a divine appointment. "He chose this trip, Sidney," I said. "And He chose you." For the first time since the trip began, a smile graced Sidney's face. I went on to tell her that Jesus loved her very much and that He wanted to help her and her daughter. "His love for you is filling my heart right now." We stood up, and I put my arms around her. "It's going to be all right," I said.

Sidney broke into tears. From that point on, her demeanor changed. The Holy Spirit had softened her heart and had done a new thing in me too. I learned that it was impossible for me to feel fear and anxiety when my heart was filled with God's love.

Chapter 23

Then he said to me, "Prophesy to the breath; prophesy, son of man, and say to it, 'This is what the Sovereign Lord says: Come from the four winds, O breath, and breathe into these slain, that they may live.'" So I prophesied as he commanded me, and breath entered them; they came to life and stood up on their feet—a vast army.

—Ezekiel 37:9-10

God blessed me with another extraordinary layover in Aruba. Before I headed to town, I took a moment of quiet time with God. I asked Him to lead me to a jewelry store that carried a particular wristwatch. I had heard that watches were significantly less expensive in Aruba, and I didn't have much time to find one.

Almost effortlessly, I found the bus shelter down the street that would take me to the shopping district. The second jewelry store I went to had the watch. It was nearly half the list retail price. Praise God!

After buying the watch, I wandered through the city and in and out of a few stores. I noticed that many of the jewelry stores had hired women to stand outside their doors and hand out flyers. All of the women I saw appeared to be poor. I wondered how much money the jewelry stores paid these women. I felt compassion for them, and I prayed for each one of them.

It didn't take long before I realized that I was on an assignment for God, walking around the district, praying and intervening for the people of Aruba. I prayed Ezekiel

37:9–10 over the island. And I found that the more I beseeched God, the more empowered I felt to do the work of Jesus.

Throughout my short layover, God blessed me with sunlight, strong breezes, and a perfect beach setting. He blessed me with delicious fine foods and equally fine service as I dined. He blessed me with His divine peace. He lifted my spirit. I felt filled and energized by the time I arrived at the airport to return to Philadelphia the following day. I was ready for His next divine appointment, for His next blessing.

It arrived in the form of three female passengers who were returning to Philadelphia from their annual Aruba vacation. As I served beverages from a cart in the coach cabin, I finished what I thought was my last row of passengers. When I began to roll the cart away, a woman on the aisle looked at me and said, "May I have something cold to drink?" This struck me as odd because she already had pretzels on her tray table, and the women on either side of her already had drinks. "Isn't the stewardess in the back bringing you a drink?" I asked.

"No," she replied.

I apologized and asked the woman what she would like. She asked me for a soda that I was out of on my cart. So I wheeled the cart to the back galley and poured a drink for her there. When I walked back up the aisle and placed the drink on her tray table, I couldn't help notice a book she had pulled out. It was *Unbroken Curses*. What's interesting about this is that, had I served the woman a drink from my cart, I would not have seen the book's title because the seat back in front of her blocked my view. But because I returned the cart to the rear galley, and then approached her from behind, the book title caught my eye right away. I sensed strongly that having initially passed over this woman for a drink was no accident and that God had ordained this divine appointment.

I introduced myself to the woman and her two daughters and asked about the book. As it turned out, the book was a Christian resource on understanding and breaking various types of spiritual curses. I shared that I was a Christian too and that God had been growing me in the area of spiritual warfare. I explained that I often pray for God to lead me to sources and resources that can teach me what He wants me to learn. I believe that this book was an answer to prayer and that God used this woman to deliver the blessing. All three women drew closer and were intrigued. They shared that they were initially scheduled on a flight the day prior and that they couldn't make the earlier flight due to sunburn. So they were rebooked on this flight.

I believe that God rerouted them specifically for this divine appointment to occur. I knew that God was encouraging me through these women. And I purchased the book the following day.

Chapter 24

. . . an angel of the Lord came down from heaven . . . His appearance was like lightning . . .

—Matthew 28:2-3

In my thirst to learn more about spiritual warfare, I brought the book, *The Battle Is the Lord's*, along with me on my three-day trip. I began reading a chapter on angels while sitting on the jump seat the first evening. After reading several pages, I paused and asked God to show me an angel just because I wanted to feel closer to Him and His spirit world. Then I continued reading until right before landing.

The next day, I picked up where I had left off in the chapter on angels. As I read on the jump seat, without warning, a very loud bang resounded through the atmosphere and through the cabin. Our Boeing 737 rocked. My eyes looked up from my book and out of the porthole beside my jump seat. The sky was dark and the clouds were unusual looking. Frankly, I wasn't sure whether the noise was a result of static discharge, lightning, or an engine loss.

Within seconds after the bang, we heard a second one that was at least as loud as the first. This time, it sounded like it was on the right side of our airplane. I turned to the stewardess who sat beside me and said, "Well, it can't be both of the engines because we're still flying." We shared a laugh, and I continued to read my book. About this time, we heard passengers get sick. There was nothing we could do for them except to pray because we couldn't get out of our seats on our approach to land.

Soon after we landed and most of the passengers deplaned, both of the pilots exited the cockpit with nervous smiles. Stephen, our copilot, announced that we had been struck by lightning twice, both times on the nose of the airplane. The first strike was on the captain's side of the nose. The second was on the copilot's. This explained why the first bang sounded like it came from the left side of the plane and the second one from the right. Stephen then said that he could see the lightning bolts zigzag right at them through their windshield and that he even ducked behind the instrument panel.

As the crew and I walked through the airplane to check for structural damage, I stopped at the bulkhead between coach and first class. There on the floor were two pennies. I picked them up, knowing that God had just given them to me as a sign. Immediately, I retrieved my book and turned to the page that I had read right before the lightning struck. This is what it said: "I believe that the elements of nature such as thunder and lightning are sometimes manifestations of God's angels."[1] I showed the excerpt to Stephen, who I knew was a Christian. He smiled, and he called his wife to tell her the news. The stewardess who had earlier sat beside me on the jump seat stood nearby and heard me read the excerpt. "Clean living," she said with a smile.

I followed the captain to the middle of the cabin and looked out over his shoulder to search for any structural damage on the wings. We didn't see any. But this gave me

---

[1] Tony Evans, The Battle Is the Lord's (Chicago: Moody Press, 1998), 103.

an opportunity to share that God was just showing me a couple of angels. The captain enjoyed the story.

Then the captain and I walked up to first class and sat with the rest of the crew. He shared a testimony from his young adult years in which his bike had been stolen. He said that God not only showed him who had stolen it, but He also allowed him to reclaim it. Yes, the captain was a believer too.

As we listened and shared, I saw how God brought all of us closer to Him through this lightning encounter. God had answered my prayer by giving me double what I had asked Him for—two angels—because if He had sent only one lightning strike we might have dismissed it as simply lightning. But He knew that if He sent two strikes in the same place, we would realize that He had done something special. I also believe that God chose this particular manifestation of angels to demonstrate to me their power and character. He knew that I would need them in the days to come.

Chapter 25

Surely he took up our infirmities and carried our sorrows . . . and by his wounds we are healed.

—Isaiah 53:4-5

Before we took off on our first leg to Charlotte, Lana confessed to me, "I recently had a couple of deaths in my family, and this is my first trip back."

My heart melted, and I felt Jesus' mercy and love for this stewardess. I asked Lana whether she believed in God. She said that she did and that she had been praying. The Holy Spirit enabled me to see that Lana was not a strong Christian and that she was not living in the will of God. "I would like to pray for you," I said. Lana stood against the galley counter and looked at me. I explained to her that I pray before every trip and ask God to give me divine appointments with others. This news brought half a smile to Lana's face.

After takeoff, I took Lana's hands and lifted her up to God. I thanked Him for this divine appointment and asked for His divine protection, comfort, and healing during Lana's vulnerable time of mourning and recovery. I asked Him to send her angels to minister to her. Lana opened her eyes and thanked me quietly.

As I stood and walked down the aisle to serve the coach cabin, I felt a peace waft over me. A great desire to praise God in His language welled up in me. The Holy Spirit revealed to me that God was demonstrating a new way to use His gift of tongues. Since I had received this gift, I had used it only when praying warfare prayers. But now, He was urging me to include praise. At this point in my walk, I had no idea that praise is actually a form of warfare. The urge to praise God was overwhelming, so I ducked into the lavatory and honored Him by praying praise back to Him.

On the second day of our trip, Lana sat on the jump seat, holding her abdomen. I assumed that she had menstrual cramps, and so I asked her whether she had taken any medicine. She didn't give me a straight answer, so I offered her ibuprofen. As she took the medicine, I began to feel righteous anger rise up in me because I sensed that at the root of her pain was evil.

"Do you really want the pain to go away?" I asked. Lana responded with a sheepish nod as her body doubled over. I placed my hands on her back, and I asked Jesus to lend His healing touch to her body, to pour divine health into her, and to give her His peace. I asked Him to use this miracle of healing to draw Lana closer to Him.

When I finished this quick prayer, I took my hands away. Lana opened her eyes and looked at me and said, "Put your hands back on me."

"What?"

"Your hands," she said. "They're hot."

I was surprised to hear this because my hands didn't feel hot to me. I put my hands up to my cheek and they were cool. So I knew that if she had felt heat it came from the Holy Spirit through me, not from me. This was a new experience for me, and I felt humbled and amazed.

I offered to pray for Lana again. "No," she replied. "The pain is going away." Within seconds, she stood up, grabbed her cosmetic bag, and went into the lavatory.

When she emerged, she had her full makeup on: lavender eye shadow, eyeliner, the works. Lana felt well enough to want to look good. The healing touch of Jesus had brought her out of her slump. I was awed by this amazing manifestation, and I felt encouraged to continue to lay hands on people.

Chapter 26

Be self-controlled and alert. Your enemy the devil prowls around like a roaring lion looking for someone to devour.

—1 Peter 5:8

Lisa voiced her upset about having received our trip from crew scheduling. She had requested a three-day trip and ours was a two-day. The same circumstances happened to Elizabeth. Both stewardesses said that they had been assigned the trip due to a contract technicality, and each of them had lost flight time. But as I listened to their laments, I was reminded of the difficulty that I experienced in trying to get to work this first morning of our trip. I ran late, which was unusual for me, and I nearly wrecked on the highway en route. One thing I knew for sure was that God was in control and that He had purposed all three of us to be here.

During our five-and-a-half-hour flight to Los Angeles, we got to know each other a little better. After our passenger service, we gathered in the rear galley. Elizabeth sat and opened her book, *Secrets of the Vine*, and I shared with her my book, *The Battle Is the Lord's*. As Elizabeth scanned through the spiritual warfare book, Lisa and I conversed. Lisa shared that her husband of two years was a US Navy pilot and that he had shipped out September 19, 2001, for a six-month assignment in the Middle East. She said that she had handed the entire issue over to the Lord and that she was not worried about him.

At the end of our flight, I stood with my luggage mid-aisle and waited for the other stewardesses to catch up. I happened to look down, and there was a "penny of encouragement." I sensed that something big would take place.

The following day, we boarded passengers onto our Boeing 757 to near capacity. Our flight was uneventful until the end of our service. As I stood in the rear galley cleaning up, I reached for a tall stack of Styrofoam cups on the countertop. What I did not see was that the top cup was filled with hot water. When I picked up the stack, the hot water spilled over my hand and wrist. I was so shocked and in so much pain that I couldn't speak. Additionally, I felt exhausted, and my back ached from having served three hundred meals over the past two days. I tried at first to fight the tears but finally broke down on the jump seat with Lisa sitting next to me. Lisa and Elizabeth tried to comfort me, but all I could do was cry and hold my finger. This was only the second time in nearly thirteen years of flying that I had cried while working a trip. The true miracle here was that I didn't even think to blame the person who had carelessly put hot water into a stack of cups that appeared to be empty, a true departure from where God had grown me a year earlier.

After I settled down, an elderly man pulled back the curtain between the galley and the coach cabin. He stuck his head in and informed us that he had been flying for thirteen hours and that he was on the verge of a panic attack.

I immediately stood up and stepped over Lisa and asked the gentleman to follow me. I shared with him that God had helped me overcome panic attacks, and I invited him to sit on one of our jump seats. He had been previously seated in a middle seat, wedged between two people. I gave him a cup of ice water and asked him to let me know if he needed oxygen. Then I gave him what he needed most: space and prayer.

I returned to the rear galley and sat down. Lisa shared that she had a problem with anxiety and that she experienced panic attacks. I shared what I had learned about panic disorder and how Satan uses it against people to make them feel out of control, as if they're dying. Lisa said that she wanted to overcome this stronghold and didn't want to resort to medicine. Lisa also shared that she had a problem with asking her husband for money and that it was creating division between them. She talked a little longer and we realized that the problem didn't have anything to do with money but rather with feeling dependent, vulnerable, and out of control. Elizabeth and I took turns counseling Lisa about holes in her faith, about how God wanted her to depend upon Him not others, that He is our all-sufficient provider, and that she could trust Him entirely. I gazed over at Elizabeth and we smiled because we knew that God had given Lisa this opportunity for healing. I asked Elizabeth to join me in laying hands on our sister. And so we did. Soon after I started praying, Lisa began to cry. After I finished, Elizabeth prayed, and Lisa cried more. When we finished, Lisa felt renewed. She said that she could feel God lifting her burdens, her lack of trust in Him, her not putting God first before herself and her husband. She knew that she was protected and headed in a new direction of faith. Elizabeth and I could see the immediate change in Lisa's relaxed eyes. Lisa then stood up and said that she wanted to talk with the man who felt panicky.

Alone in the rear galley, Elizabeth confessed to me that she struggled with a fear of praying publicly, that this was her first time openly praying for someone. I shared with her that I, too, used to have those fears and that God had broken that stronghold of fear off of me, just as He had in her.

Lisa returned to the galley and began chattering about the man who had felt panicky. She said that he was a retired military officer and medical doctor and that he was currently a travel writer. Lisa seemed to have found a new energy.

After we deplaned, Lisa, Elizabeth, and I walked to another concourse to pick up our next airplane, a Boeing 767. This would be the final leg of our trip back to Philadelphia. As we sat in the gate area awaiting the aircraft's arrival, I searched through my Bible cover pocket for a spiritual warfare prayer to give to Lisa. I didn't find it, but I did find a printed web page from a well-known ministry. It was a devotional about anxiety. Another stewardess had given it to me long ago, and I had forgotten about it. I pulled it out and handed it to Lisa. This prompted Elizabeth to pull out her Bible study workbook on ministering to others. She turned to a page about anxiety. There were definitions and scriptures that backed up our prayer session with Lisa. Elizabeth handed the workbook over to Lisa and asked her to look at it. There was a single scripture that the Holy Spirit illuminated to Lisa, Matthew 6:33: "But seek first his kingdom and his righteousness, and all these things will be given to you as well." Lisa knelt down in front of us, the workbook in hand, and said, "I had this scripture read at my wedding. How could I have forgotten this? It is so important. I haven't been putting Him first."

"You were supposed to be on this trip so that He could remind you," I said. Elizabeth smiled and nodded. She then pulled out a worn plastic bag full of little booklets, each touching on an area in which Elizabeth was struggling. They encompassed loneliness, low self-esteem, satanic attacks, and others. Elizabeth handed them to me and said that they were her "life-blood library." I was touched that she would share the most intimate and vulnerable part of herself with me.

We boarded the passengers, served the short flight, and said our good-byes. Lisa promised to give us an update on her relationship with her husband and her walk with God. I knew that the next time I crossed paths with either of these women I would feel a sisterly closeness.

The next day, I woke up at home in my own bed. As I readied myself for the day, the Holy Spirit enlightened me on how Satan can get a grip on me when I leave my house a little late for work. He can shake me up in traffic and throw me into a frantic frenzy. I thought about how I almost missed that first flight two days earlier, and how I could've missed out on a very important assignment, one that affected other people's lives, not just my own. I also realized that God delivered me to that flight despite my tardiness, not because I deserved it, but because He had a mission to accomplish through me, which I had prayed to receive, one that Satan couldn't prevent.

Four months later, I crossed paths with Lisa while switching aircraft. As she pulled her luggage past me in the aisle, she greeted me and said that she hadn't had a panic attack since she received prayer on our flight. I felt so blessed that God provided this encouraging evidence of healing, and I thanked Him.

Chapter 27

Preach the Word; be prepared in season and out of season; correct, rebuke and encourage—with great patience and careful instruction.

—2 Timothy 4:2

As we waited in the hotel lobby for Toni to join us for dinner, Keisha and I listened to Captain Chuck boldly present his viewpoint on the Muslim religion and September 11. He declared that all religions had been debased, including Christianity. As I watched Chuck speak, God showed me much through His gift of discernment. Chuck went on to profess that he was superior to ninety-five percent of the people he had met in his lifetime. As Chuck spoke, God continued to show me how Satan had twisted this man's mind and spirit.

At the right moment, I spoke up. "I'm a 'Jesus freak,'" I interjected. "A born-again Christian. And my perspective is very different from yours."

Chuck proceeded to raise questions, such as why were certain books left out of the Bible and whether I'd read the Dead Sea scrolls. I informed him that I had read excerpts from the Scrolls as well as from *The Koran* and that I believe God is sovereign over everything, including the writing of the *Holy Bible*. As I spoke, I felt God's peace and grace being released from within my spirit. Because of God, Chuck never ruffled my feathers; he never got to me. Instead, as I looked into his eyes, God enabled me to see a man who was captured in bondage. I knew the right thing to do was to pray for him.

As we continued to wait for Toni, Chuck continued to profess his viewpoint, citing scientific theories and facts from how the earth was created to how people receive knowledge psychically. By now, we had waited several minutes, and it seemed that Toni wasn't going to show. We stewardesses decided to get going, and Chuck chose to retreat back to his room. God's divine appointment for Keisha and me was about to be revealed, even though Satan tried to use Chuck to detour us.

Keisha and I headed onto the resort's brick path that would lead us to a road behind the hotel. Just a few blocks into the night climate, we arrived at an elegant, open-air restaurant situated in a cove setting. Keisha sparkled in her tropical dress and gold lamé slides that were illuminated by tiny white lights on nearby trees. Barbados was never more beautiful.

We ordered squash soup and flying fish. As we waited for our food, we conversed about God, a likely subject to begin with since Chuck had already opened this door. I shared my personal testimony with Keisha, saying that I had accepted Jesus into my heart when I was a teenager but that, for years, I had allowed myself to be misguided and fall away from church. I explained that, a few years ago, God had spoken to me saying, "Get in My Word!" Thereafter, I returned to church and began to study the Bible. I shared that since I had returned to church, God had grown me and blessed me. I informed Keisha that I pray before every trip, asking God to choose a trip for me, to choose each crew member according to His will, and to use me for His purpose. "He chose you," I said, "and He brought us together."

Keisha looked at me deeply, and her disposition became even more eager. She revealed that she had felt hopeless since September 11, when she lost her friend in one of the terrorist attacks and when the international route she so enjoyed working was put on hold. Keisha and I shared information about our home lives, our upbringings, and our relationship with the Lord. The more I revealed, the more she revealed about herself, her marriage, her outlook, and where she was spiritually. Several times, Keisha admitted where she needed help. She said she still felt racked with guilt over leaving her children to fly trips when they were small. She mentioned how unhappy she was in her marriage to a man who resists God.

"I can see Jesus in you," I said. Keisha confirmed that she had received Jesus in her heart but that she had fallen away. She mentioned how her husband continued to influence her in negative ways by socializing in circles of people who focused on materialism. She expressed that she was sick of the facades and that none of it fed her heart. I shared how returning to church after several years of not having a home church opened my eyes and my heart to the goodness of God through His people, how witnessing the congregation's works and relationship with the Lord warmed my heart, how going on a mission and attending my ladies Bible study brought me the intimacy in relationships that I had always craved.

As Keisha spoke, the Holy Spirit brought to my mind a tape on the topic of hope that I had tucked into my tote weeks earlier. It was one that I had intended to deliver to someone else's mailbox but was unsuccessful at finding the box. I realized now that the Spirit wanted me to give it to Keisha.

After dinner, Keisha invited me to walk on the beach next to the hotel. There I shared a little about the laying on of hands and healing. Keisha pointed out a profound curve in her spine. The curvature was so pronounced that it made the zipper in her sundress visibly crooked. I shared with Keisha how sickness and guilt are tools of Satan, how God was using me for spiritual warfare. "This must be why I'm here," she said exuberantly. "I need to learn this." Keisha talked more and more, revealing areas in which she wanted growth and clarity. As she spoke, God enabled her to see where she had fallen away and how Satan had used pockets of confusion and lack of knowledge against her. Keisha was delighted that there was hope in her darkness. She confessed that she was ready for a change. We agreed to meet back in my room for prayer.

As I opened my door for Keisha, she immediately recognized the scent of anointing oil. I had made a list of the issues that concerned her and had laid it on the coffee table in front of us, along with my Bible and the oil. The Holy Spirit guided me to invite Keisha to confess to the Lord that she had fallen away and to repent. He also led me to encourage her to ask the Holy Spirit to make known to her any unknown sins so that she could confess them and be a clean vessel before Him. Keisha agreed.

I retrieved my Bible and turned to Luke 10:19 and read aloud how God gives His Christians authority to trample on the plans Satan has against them. God worked through me to show Keisha how to rebuke Satan when he comes against her and how to use the authority of Jesus Christ to send him away. Then I handed her a warfare prayer, the one that Marge had shared with me months earlier. And I wrote down a protection prayer for her, the same one that God had taught me through Barbara, also months earlier.

After Keisha confessed and repented, I took the oil, dabbed it onto my fingers and made a cross on her spine. I took authority over Satan operating in her life, commanding him to depart, and breaking all his plans against her. I claimed the blood of Jesus over her and the power of the cross in her life. I prayed healing and protection over her. I asked for God to send angels to minister to her and to extend His discernment and wisdom to her. I affirmed that God had given Keisha a spirit of love and of a sound mind. I asked God to bestow His hope and divine love, His peace and confidence and blessings over her, and for Him to give her a renewed mind and healed heart. I prayed for her husband and her two children, that God would work in each of their lives, giving them a desire to seek Jesus and to know Him. I thanked God again for this divine appointment and for enabling me to accomplish His work.

The following day, Keisha and I stood in the boarding area and waited for the security check to be completed on our airplane. Keisha pulled a small, white object from her pocket. "Here," she said to me, "this is for you." I took the tiny object from her and held it in my palm. It was a shell, one that Keisha had found on the beach earlier that morning. My heart was blessed.

Once on the airplane, I walked to the rear galley and discovered that there was a problem with the escape slide cover. I called Chuck on the intercom and notified him. When he came back to check it, he apologized to me for his behavior the previous evening. He said that he believed in the free will of people to believe what they wanted. I told him that neither his honesty nor his debate skills offended me and that I knew that we were in different places due to the choices we had made. Chuck smiled and seemed fine with my response. I knew that God had answered my prayer to convict Chuck's heart.

After our flight service, Toni and I sat in the aft galley and ate dinner together. She shared a recent experience with me, saying that on her flight from Washington, DC to San Francisco two men, who were assigned first-class seats, gave them up to a woman and her baby. The reason for their kindness and generosity was that the woman was returning home from having just buried her military husband. He had been killed in Afghanistan.

I asked Toni whether she attended church. She said that she hadn't been entirely happy with the last church she attended and that she had given up her search. I shared with her my own church-search experience, how uplifting the music was to my soul, and how my heart was fed by the loving-kindness of its members. I knew that a seed had been planted.

Meanwhile, Keisha was seated on the forward jump seat reading two Christian books that I had lent to her during our five-hour flight. "Maybe this is why I left my library book on the plane yesterday," she said. "God wanted me to read these instead."

In God's perfect timing, the flight came to an end. Once on the ground in Philadelphia, the intercom rang. It was Chuck. "We got a prime gate, girls," he said. "Not that remote spot we were expecting."

"What kind of voodoo did you do to get that, Chuck?" Toni asked.

"Oh no," I said, laughing. "It wasn't voodoo. It was God's favor."

Chuck laughed.

Once at the gate, I stepped onto the Jetway where Chuck stood with his luggage and a smirk on his face. "I'm praying for you," I told him, smiling.

"God will have to work hard to change me."

"Oh, I think He's up for the challenge."

Keisha and I headed up the Jetway together. "I'm going to miss you," she said.

"I'm going to miss you too," I replied.

Keisha was scheduled to return to her international route a couple of weeks later.

Chapter 28

The Lord works righteousness and justice for all the oppressed.

—Psalm 103:6

A fter I prayed and anointed the airplane, I checked the emergency equipment and returned to first class to chat with the crew. Terri, the head stewardess, introduced herself and immediately identified herself as one of the crew members who had undergone a humiliating detoxification procedure from a potential anthrax contamination on an aircraft a couple of months after the terrorist bombings. I had briefly heard of this story from a third party weeks earlier, as news traveled fast at the airline.

Terri shared her entire story: She said that she and eleven other crew members worked a Boeing 757 flight to Ft. Lauderdale. During the flight, another stewardess found a liquor kit containing a large amount of powdery substance. She notified the other crew members and the decision was made to contact MedLink, a medical emergency consultation service.

When the plane landed in Ft. Lauderdale, all of the passengers deplaned, except the crew. Officials from various government agencies then stormed the plane, including the FBI, Hazardous Materials, and a sheriff. The crew was informed that they were required to undergo a detoxification procedure. They were then instructed to leave all their baggage and belongings on the aircraft and deplane two-by-two. The pilots went first.

When each of the pairs deplaned, they were informed to take off all of their clothes, right on the tarmac. Stewardesses cried. The Hazardous Materials authorities then proceeded to scrub the crew member's bodies. According to Terri, they used a dirty-like, paint-style bucket with dingy rags and bleach water. After scrubbing them from head to toe, they rinsed them down with garden-type hoses spouting cold water from the airport spigot. Terri said that both men and women stood and watched and scrubbed the stewardesses as her head was pushed under the garden hose repeatedly to the point that she had to jerk her head back to catch her breath.

After she was hosed down, Terri was handed a small towel, no bigger than a kitchen paper towel. Then she was handed a paper jumpsuit, which she struggled to pull onto her damp body. By the time she got it on, the jumpsuit was soaked, and it became transparent.

Finally, a representative from the airline showed up and offered the crew navy blue sweat suits. After donning the sweats, the crew was interrogated, then debriefed, then herded onto a van to a local hotel. When they arrived, the hotel clerks had already seen the television news coverage concerning the situation and refused to offer them rooms. The airline representative finally convinced them that the crew was not a threat. He also offered his credit card at the front desk so that the crew could eat. Their wallets, hairbrushes, hair dryers, shoes, underwear, jewelry, cell phones, medicines, and other personal items remained with the authorities and wouldn't be delivered until the following morning.

Once in the hotel room, Terri telephoned her ex-husband, who was a judge in Tennessee. From him, Terri learned that during wartime the government can do anything, including strip workers down naked in a public area, touch them, and hose them off with cold water, then force them to wear see-through jumpsuits.

Terri said that, when morning came, the crew decided to meet for a buffet breakfast at the hotel. They showed up with their sweats, bare feet, and uncombed hair. When they wanted to get in line at the buffet, the company representative spoke up and insisted that they sit in a corner of the restaurant and appear as inconspicuous as possible. He promised that food would be brought to them.

At some point, according to Terri, union representatives showed up and spoke with the crew. Later, they would send out letters advising and warning other airlines about this incident. But for now, they promised the crew that this would never happen again.

During our final flight of the day, I was able to speak with Terri alone. I asked her what went through her mind from a spiritual perspective. Terri said that she believed that her body was a temple of God and that she felt violated. She said that it was very emotional. "Can you imagine my fifty-year-old body out there on that ramp naked?" she asked. She said she asked God to show her a purpose for the incident, to show her how to use it to help others. And then we prayed.

Chapter 29

Surely he will save you from the fowler's snare and from
the deadly pestilence.

—Psalm 91:3

I recognized Captain John from having flown with him
before. As he briefed the crew prior to our trip, I noticed
that he seemed a bit more intense than I remembered him
being, particularly on the issue of terrorism. It didn't take
long to see why. Almost immediately, he shared a couple
of stories with me that revealed an ounce of the responsi-
bility that weighed upon his shoulders.

John said that he had been notified by his chief pilot
that the FBI intercepted a bomb threat over a Yahoo e-mail.
The threat concerned a specific flight that John was scheduled to work on the second day of his trip. John said that
the chief pilot assured him that many precautions would
be taken, including on-board air marshals, aircraft bomb
searches with dogs, and the scanning of all one hundred-
plus passengers.

On the day his trip began, John met the stewardesses
who would work the trip with him. He said that none of
them had been notified of the bomb threat and that they
were alarmed at the news.

On the second day of the trip, the crew showed up
at the Seattle airport, and administrative chaos ensued.
John was informed that there would be no air marshals
on the flight after all. The station manager at the airport
suggested to John that only a small percentage of passengers be scanned in an effort to get the flight out on time.

Meanwhile, company administrators were contacted concerning what to inform the passengers when they would, understandably, ask why they were being rescanned with a wand at the gate. According to John, one of the vice presidents of our airline said to tell the passengers anything as long as no one mentioned a bomb threat. In addition to this folly, the Transportation Safety Administration (TSA), which was new at the time, was contacted in a last ditch effort to secure air marshals for the flight. John said that the TSA refused to authorize air marshals for them and also refused to put such a statement in writing. With this, the safety director for our airline was contacted, who, ultimately, canceled the flight. John and his crew then ferried their empty Airbus 321, which, at capacity, holds 169 passengers, back to Charlotte.

The second incident John shared with me occurred around the same time as the first. It involved a couple of passengers who behaved suspiciously after boarding a flight. The stewardesses felt uncomfortable with the passengers' behavior and asked that they be removed from the aircraft. After removing the passengers, authorities scanned them and found what John described as a "big knife" on one of them. John proved his point: that there were potential terrorists who were still out there flying around, casing us for soft spots in our security.

Understandably, I felt alarmed to hear about these incidents. John and the rest of our crew and I were scheduled to fly to LAX on the second day of our trip, which would be five days after the fatal shootings at the El Al ticket counter.

When the second day arrived, we were given no air marshals on our Charlotte to Los Angeles flight. I thought this was odd since we had transported two of them out of Houston to Charlotte with us, just hours earlier, and since we were flying into LAX so recently after the shooting. Still, God watched over us, and the flight was uneventful.

Afterwards during my quiet time with God, the Holy Spirit revealed to me that, although I had been praying prayers of protection over our airplanes, our crews, and our passengers, I was not specifically praying for protection against terrorism. He also revealed to me that I still carried unconfessed animosity toward former CEOs and presidents of the airline, blaming them for the airline's weak financial foundation. The Holy Spirit convicted me and spoke to me saying that I should ask God to get the airline back into a healthy financial position and to protect us against terrorism. God had been developing me in the areas of warfare and healing people. Now it was time to include the airline.

Chapter 30

And pray in the Spirit on all occasions with all kinds of prayers and requests. With this in mind, be alert and always keep on praying for all the saints.

—Ephesians 6:18

As I prayed for safe flights and financial security, God continued to reveal accounts of weaknesses in both areas.

In one such case, a captain on one of my trips shared a story about a man who feigned loosing his wallet in-flight. When the man called a stewardess over and asked to speak to an authority on board, she responded wisely. She informed the man that the captain would speak to him after the aircraft landed. The man then "found" his wallet on the floor and asked the stewardess to disregard his request. The captain believed that the man staged this episode in an attempt to learn whether authorities were aboard.

As I continued to pray for safe flights, I noticed that there seemed to be an increased number of air marshals traveling the flights that I worked. While I had an opportunity one day, I asked one of them what the reason was for the increase. "One captain told me that he thought there were more potential terrorists out there who continued to case our planes in search of holes in our security," I said. The air marshal was silent for a moment. Then he looked at me, raised an eyebrow, and said very succinctly, "You need to pay attention to that."

As I continued to pray for the airline's financial security, an Airline Pilots Association (ALPA) representative boarded my flight one day and greeted me. I had flown with this union representative/pilot before, and I knew him casually. He looked weary from the many negotiations and from commuting from his hometown to work. He informed me that the airline would announce hundreds more furloughs the next day. Sure enough, the furloughs were announced on time, within days after the airline filed for chapter 11 protection.

As I continued to pray for safe flights and the airline's financial security, a man on one of my flights handed another stewardess a plastic bag full of lapel pins along with his business card and a note. The stewardess handed me one of the pins from the bag saying that it was a gift from a passenger. His note informed us that he was a paratrooper in the US Army Reserve and that he would be willing to help us in any way. I pinned the tiny symbol of the United States, which was embellished with stars and stripes and "9/11/01," onto my lapel. In the meantime, the other stewardess moved the paratrooper and his wife up to the first-class cabin as an expression of our appreciation. I walked over to the man, shook his hand, and thanked him. He smiled, nodded out of respect, and replied, "I know you have a thankless job. So do I. I work for the post office. I understand, and I wanted to say thank you." I knew in my spirit that God was pleased with me and that He sent this man to express this.

Chapter 31

May the Lord Jesus Christ . . . encourage your hearts
and strengthen you in every good deed and word.
                                    —2 Thessalonians 2:16-17

During my first time cooking and preparing meals in
the first-class galley of an Airbus 321, I was relieved
to find that Tyler, the head steward, was patient with me.
We had to work together in close quarters, and it probably
helped that his wife had given birth to their first child, a
girl, just twelve weeks prior to our trip. He was on top of
the world.

Orlando had always been a favorite destination of mine
to work because the children on the flights brought such
joy to my heart. This particular flight seemed blessed from
the start. Although it was oversold by several seats, the
passengers were amazingly patient as they boarded. One
family offered to hold their ticketed two-year-old child in
their lap so that someone else could take his seat. I had
never witnessed so much kindness and generosity on a
flight before. Another family with two small boys offered
to stay behind and take a later flight so that others could
have their seats. Even the aircraft cleaners were kind and
generous in that they kept returning with whatever sup-
plies we needed throughout the boarding process.

With this, Tyler and I stood in the forward entrance
and looked at each other in amazement. "Must've been
those prayers I prayed," I said to him, smiling. I knew in
my heart that God had answered my prayers for a peaceful
flight and for us to see the face of Jesus in each other. Tyler

looked at me pensively and confessed that he had begun to think about God since his daughter's birth. I knew a seed had been planted.

After our service, I headed toward the coach cabin to help pick up trash. As I passed by a little girl sitting in first class, I noticed that she was concentrating on drawing a picture. I continued down the aisle and thought nothing more of it.

Toward the end of the flight, Tyler handed me the girl's artwork and said to me, "A little girl drew this for us." I took the picture in my hands. It was an illustration of an outdoor scene, including a tree, a sun, red flowers, birds, an azure sky, and a house. The note inside read, "To the flight attendants: Thank you for helping me." Nothing could have been sweeter.

God, indeed, cares about the little things. I truly believe that He worked through this little girl to demonstrate His presence. I sensed that He was pleased with me for obeying Him, for bringing Him to work, for praying for passengers, for planting seeds.

What's more, the blue marker that the little girl used to draw the sky and to write the words "Thank you" was the perfect shade that I had been seeking to paint a wall in my living room. For months, I had searched for just the right shade of blue without success. Now I could take the drawing with me to the paint store. I was indeed blessed.

Chapter 32

. . . On him we have set our hope that he will continue
to deliver us, as you help us by your prayers.
—2 Corinthians 1:10-11

My stewardess friend, Donna, knew that I prayed before trips, asking God to choose one for me and to
choose every other crew member. Donna knew that she
was supposed to be on this particular trip. Connor, a dear
pal with whom I had flown before, also worked with us.

As we approached Pittsburgh that day, lightning struck
our plane. I heard a nervous passenger in seat 1A, directly
behind the bulkhead in front of me, gag loudly and vomit.
Even though I felt my senses surge to a heightened awareness, I was not afraid because I knew that God was in control. He had a purpose, and I was confident that He would
reveal His purpose to me.

Once we landed, I stood by the exit door and waited
for the gate agent to knock. As I waited in the quiet, a passenger stood next to me and said, "Praise God."

"You're a believer too?" I asked.

"Yes," he replied.

"I pray over each airplane I'm on," I said to him. "I
even anoint them with oil." The passenger said that he was
glad to know that crews pray.

Once the passengers deplaned, the captain stepped out
onto the Jetway to confer with a mechanic. He informed
the mechanic that he didn't know whether the plane had
been struck by lightning or whether it had discharged
static.

"It was lightning," I said. "The passenger in 3F saw it hit the right engine."

The mechanic and the captain looked at me, but the captain never acknowledged my words otherwise. He only said, "There wasn't any indication on radar or any reports of lightning."

"That's how God works," I thought. "Otherwise, we would just pass the strike off as a force of nature, devoid of His intervention."

While boarding our next flight, bound for Montreal, a woman walked on in tears. When I asked her whether she was all right, she cried even harder. I opened the lavatory door, grabbed a handful of tissues, and handed them to her. She walked close to me in the forward galley and mumbled that she didn't know where her seat was located. When I asked her for her boarding pass, she cried even harder and buried her head in my left shoulder. I knew then that whatever was happening within this woman was big, and so I hugged her. After a moment, I assured her that I had a special seat just for her. I knew that the front row of first class was available, and I escorted the woman there. She thanked me and then asked me for a hard drink.

About this time, Donna walked up the aisle and saw the woman's tote on the floor in front of her feet. Donna stowed the bag for the woman and then whispered to me that inside the woman's open tote were medical x-rays.

During the flight, I approached the distressed woman and sat in the seat next to her. "Would you like to talk?" I asked. The woman looked at me with sad eyes. She could barely speak. In between sobs, the woman managed to say that her husband was dying of cancer and that she very recently learned that his prognosis was eight months. She introduced herself as Betty.

"Do you believe in God?" I asked.

Betty paused and stared at me with her big, sad eyes. "Yes," she replied.

Then a question came into my mind that I knew was not from me: "Do you go to church?"

Betty responded with an even longer pause. "I used to," she said. She explained that she ceased going to church two years ago when her first husband and their son both died.

For a second, I was at a loss for words. "I think I understand how you feel," I said. And then I shared with her my testimony, that, years earlier, I had lost two relatives to lung cancer almost simultaneously and that my father also struggled with lung cancer at that same time. I explained how I cried out to God in desperation to spare my father. "He did," I said. "He spared him." I explained to her that God had given us this divine appointment, that He had placed both her and me on this particular flight. "He wants you to reconcile with Him so that He can help you," I said.

Betty looked at me, silent for a moment. Then she said, "I want to do that."

I took Betty's hands in mine, and I asked her to relax. Then I began to pray. I thanked God for this divine appointment and for His mercy and grace to receive Betty again. Then I pled the blood of Jesus over Betty and asked for His divine purpose and will in her life. I asked for a miracle of healing for her husband. Then I suggested to Betty that she pour out her heart in repentance.

As I prayed, I sensed that other passengers could hear me. A couple of them even walked past me en route to the lavatory. As I felt our plane descend, I hugged Betty and then excused myself to secure the galley for landing.

Donna rejoined me on our jump seat. Immediately, she began to cry and complain about how Connor treated her during the flight. I could hardly absorb Donna's laments because I was saturated with Betty's issues and the lightning strike. So I prayed silently to God and asked Him for His strength to endure my friend's cries and to help her.

The Holy Spirit enabled me to see that Donna felt overly sensitive because of old wounds. I suggested to her that she "chase" after Jesus' healing. Then I explained to Donna that sometimes others don't see our strengths. They only see our wounds, and when they see our wounds they tend to respond accordingly, depending on where they are in their spiritual walk.

After landing, I gave Betty my e-mail address and a big, long hug. Thereafter, our crew deplaned, and we headed to Canadian customs. Betty stood at the head of a long line of passengers, and I sensed that she had been searching for me in the crowd. I walked up to her and hugged her again. She held me for a long time. Both of us ended up passing through customs simultaneously, and we met on the other side. The Holy Spirit reminded me how vulnerable and lost I felt when I had relatives dying of a terminal illness. So I guided Betty on how to retrieve her luggage and how to pass through the next checkpoint. Then I hugged her again and rejoined my crew.

That evening in my hotel room I telephoned my friend, Evelyn, a mature Christian sister. Before I could share Betty's story with Evelyn, she began to tell me what happened. She said that the Holy Spirit showed her that I had prayed for a woman on an airplane. Evelyn could even see where Betty was originally assigned to sit. The Spirit showed Evelyn that other passengers overheard my prayer for Betty. "This was part of God's plan," she said.

I felt exuberant to hear these confirmations. Then I told Evelyn about the lightning. She said that the Holy Spirit revealed to her the lightning was a demonstration that He was in control. The next day, I shared this information with Donna.

About a month later, I received e-mail from Betty's daughter, thanking me for assisting her mother. Her note reminded me to continue to pray for Betty and her family, for God to provide for her, to lead her back to church, and for her to walk closely with Him.

I also received a telephone call from Donna. Through tears, she shared that she had experienced a breakthrough during communion at her church. She said that the Holy Spirit spoke to her, asking her whether she understood that Jesus' body was broken for her. I knew then that God had used me as an intercessor to bring breakthrough to these women, and I was grateful.

Chapter 33

Humble yourselves before the Lord, and he will lift you up.

—James 4:10

Summer had just returned to work after a medical leave of absence. She showed me a scar on her right knee where a surgeon had inserted a screw to repair her broken leg. This latest affliction, however, which was caused by a fall taken on the crew parking lot bus, was not the worst one she had suffered during the past year. Summer wept as she shared that she had also recovered from a double mastectomy and a hysterectomy. She explained that both of these surgeries were precautionary due to her family's extensive history of deadly female cancers.

During the few times that I had flown with Summer, she had shared family dilemmas, but nothing like this. A Catholic, she said that she still hadn't attended Mass since I had last flown with her but she wanted to. She cited the reason as being a lack of trust in God to protect her children from priest pedophiles. She mentioned how lovely it would have been to have had the assistance of a church family during her recovery, as none of her relatives lived nearby.

As I listened to Summer's extraordinary circumstances, the Holy Spirit moved within me, and I felt an overwhelming desire to pray for her. I had learned, from having previously flown with her, that God had led other Christians to her for the purpose of witnessing and that one of them had been a former Catholic. Summer and I agreed to meet in her hotel room for prayer.

Once there, we discussed her spiritual walk with Jesus, generational curses, and satanic attacks. We discussed forgiveness, trust, faith, and repentance. We discussed the blood covenant of Jesus, divine protection, and restoration. We discussed the critical importance of praise and worship. And we prayed and prayed and prayed. The Holy Spirit moved, and Summer accepted Christ into her heart.

As we finished flying our trip together, Summer's spirit seemed lighter. Ironically, most of the flights that we worked were light too. Of them, only one was full. I believe God knew she needed a break.

Days after our trip ended, God gave Summer and me another divine appointment. She had just finished two days of annual training and was returning home on a flight that I was working. "I did that thing you told me," she said. I had no idea what Summer was talking about. "You know that 'face' thing," she said. Summer then placed her palms together and her right cheek on them. Suddenly, I got it. What Summer referred to was praying on her face. When we had met previously in her hotel room, I had suggested that she continue to humble herself and seek the Lord on her face. I was delighted to know that she had followed through. Her humility touched my heart and encouraged me. And I knew that God would bless her.

Chapter 34

I want you to know, brothers, that the gospel I preached
is not something that man made up.

—Galatians 1:11

When I walked down the Jetway and first saw Jill, I sensed that God had made a divine appointment for us. I could not help but overhear her telephone conversation as I passed by. I noticed that, as she spoke, she used God's name as an exclamation at the end of her sentences. I had never met Jill before, and although I didn't know what kind of religious beliefs she held, I discerned that they weren't Christian.

Once I walked on board, Jill returned to the aircraft. We introduced ourselves briefly before she plopped down in a first-class seat and struck up a conversation with the other stewardess. As Jill spoke about her psychotherapist, the Holy Spirit demonstrated to me that I needed to use a subtle approach with her. So during our first day of flying, I built a rapport with Jill.

On the second and final day of our trip, I prayed for God to give me an uninterrupted opportunity to talk and pray with her. God knew that He had grown my faith and boldness to a point where He had enabled me to feel confident in witnessing to someone I had never met. Frankly, I was a little surprised that He had so much confidence in me.

After serving our second flight of the day, Jill sat down on the jump seat beside me. It was the first time during our trip that she had done so. I sensed that she had warmed up to me since the beginning of the trip and that she had been so consumed with her personal issues earlier that she didn't have space for anyone or anything new.

We began to talk, and I shared that I was about to embark on premarital counseling. Then I asked her about her therapist. This opened a door of common ground and ignited Jill's enthusiasm. From her tote, she retrieved two books that she said her therapist had recommended to her. The book covers suggested to me that they each contained a New Age slant. Jill handed the books to me and proceeded to open up about her life. She said that she had gotten divorced about three years earlier and that the divorce was caused by choices she had made. Jill said that she was determined to get herself straightened out before dating anyone else.

I skimmed through one of Jill's books and read a couple of chapters. Sure enough, the book was what I had suspected: a New Age amalgam of philosophies. Among them, I detected influences from Catholicism, Native American beliefs, and eastern religions.

After serving our next leg, Jill sat beside me again. I shared that I was Christian. Then I pulled out *The Battle Is the Lord's* from my tote and turned to the section on pantheism.[2] I informed Jill that I had some concerns about the book she was reading. I explained to her that Satan is the father of all lies and that Satan tries to hook people into his lies by telling them just enough of the truth to pique their interest. "If we don't know God's truth," I said, "which is His Word, we can become misled."

Jill listened intently as I confessed to her that I, myself, had at one time been spiritually misled and off track,

---

[2] Ibid., 179.

dabbling in New Age-isms, all the while thinking it was harmless fun. I shared with her that God is love and that He alone is the one true power source, all that we need.

Jill nodded as I shared that I had prayed before our trip and had asked God to choose a trip and a divine appointment for me. I told her that I believed the divine appointment was between her and me and that I wanted to pray for her.

Jill was receptive. As I began to pray for her, the Holy Spirit gave me the word "forgiveness" and told me that God desired Jill to forgive herself for having made choices that contributed to the demise of her marriage. "Have you forgiven yourself?" I asked.

Jill gazed pensively ahead at the wall of cabinets in front of us. She shook her head and said, "No, I don't think so."

I explained to her that through Jesus Christ we are forgiven for our sins and how important it was for her to accept Him and forgive herself, so that she would no longer walk in guilt.

Jill seemed relieved. I advised her to stop reading her books and to trade her counselor in for a Christian counselor. I encouraged Jill to get in line with God's powerful love and will for her life. Jill thanked me for my forthrightness and honesty, but she still wasn't ready to fully accept the Lord. So I prayed and asked Him to continue to guide her steps and to send strong Christians to help her.

Chapter 35

Therefore confess your sins to each other and pray for each other so that you may be healed. The prayer of a righteous man is powerful and effective.

—James 5:16

Since I had flown with Marissa before, I knew her to be a quiet and easy-going woman, the mother of two children, and a Christian. I knew something was up when, during the first day of our trip, she commented, "My husband is driving me crazy." I didn't see much of her during our first day of flying, because I worked first class and she worked coach. So I prayed that God would provide a quiet, uninterrupted time for us to talk.

The time arrived early on our second and final day of the trip. We had a three-plus-hour layover at the Philadelphia airport where Marissa and I had lunch together. As we sat down, we immediately began a conversation about the topic of marriage. It didn't take long before Marissa confessed that her husband, Sonny, had a drinking issue.

She said that the drinking issue had caused trauma to her daughter, especially, and that she didn't even want to call home during her trips because she couldn't bear to hear her daughter's cries. Marissa also explained that she and her husband were leaders in their church and that she had tried to hide his drinking from the church. She said that once, when their pastor's wife had visited their house and Marissa went into the garage to retrieve something for her, she was afraid the pastor's wife would follow her into the garage and discover Sonny's hiding place for his cases of beer. Marissa said that she was afraid her husband would kill her if he learned she had told anyone.

As Marissa spoke, desperation and fear laced her voice and her facial expressions. As I listened, I knew why God chose me to hear her story. God had surely grown within me a heart of compassion in this area, as I, too, had known this type of pain. I encouraged Marissa by sharing my own testimony with her and suggesting that Jesus was her escape. I knew that, by her simply confessing this family secret to me, she had opened a door to freedom from fear, shame, and isolation. I also knew that God was using the circumstances of my past to help her and the same God who set me free would set her free.

After lunch, Marissa and I walked over to a corner of a vacant boarding area, which God graciously provided, and we prayed. I held Marissa's hands, and we thanked God for our divine appointment, and then we lifted up Marissa and her family. Through our authority in Christ, we confessed and broke the curse of alcoholism and asked God for His protection. We invited Jesus to come in and lead this family out of all darkness. We asked Him to heal Marissa and her family, to mend their broken hearts, renew their minds, and to refresh their spirits.

Marissa cried as we prayed. I knew she was relieved that God had answered her desperate plea for help. Marissa confessed that she had been holding onto the Book of Philippians, saying that it had helped her to get through anything.

Six months after this divine appointment, I crossed paths with Marissa in the Philadelphia airport. We hugged, and she said that she had something to share. She whispered in my ear that her husband had not taken a drink since we prayed together. We leaped with joy at what God had surely done.

Chapter 36

Jesus stopped and called them. "What do you want me to do for you?" he asked.

—Matthew 20:32

For some time now, God had been developing me in the area of healing. He had connected me with books, tapes, conferences, and people to train me. He had connected me with people to pray for inside and outside of airplanes. Frequently, I had anointed people with oil and prayed over them to be healed. Having had these experiences gave me confidence in this anointing. I had reached a point of boldness. And then God put Luke on my flight.

Luke sat in the first row of first class with his assist dog at his feet. During our flight, I chatted with him about his visual impairment, and he shared that he had been blind from birth. "Do you believe in God?" I asked him.

"Yes," he replied.

I informed Luke that I would like to pray for God to restore his eyesight.

"I don't want that," he said.

I was shocked. Never before had anyone told me that they did not want to be healed. I was silent for a moment. And then I said, "Is there anything that I may pray for you?"

"Yes," Luke replied. "Pray for good 'vibes.'" Luke explained that he was traveling to a job interview.

I walked into the forward galley where another stewardess stood, and I explained to her what had just happened.

She replied that perhaps since Luke had never known sight, he was afraid to be healed. I felt overwhelmed.

There were many other passengers on that flight who could have benefited from prayer. One woman sat in the mid-section of coach attached to an oxygen tank. Her lips were white, and her neck and chest were adorned with several cross pendants and angel pins. Another woman, who sat at the coach bulkhead, had had a foot amputated due to diabetes. My heart broke as I watched her walk in front of me on her stub en route to the lavatory.

I wanted to walk down the aisle and reach out and touch all the sick people and pray for them. But after talking with Luke, my heart was heavy with discouragement. I felt like crying, and I didn't know what to do. So I prayed for God to help me, and then I silently prayed for the afflicted passengers.

After this trip ended, God spoke to me through His Word one morning. I had been reading the gospels as the Holy Spirit had instructed me to do. Then I came upon Matthew 20:32, in which Jesus asks, "What do you want me to do for you?" Through this scripture and others, I saw that in each case where Jesus healed people, they wanted it. And in each case, the afflicted clearly conveyed what they wanted. Nothing was presumed by Jesus. God showed me that I had presumed that Luke wanted to see, when, in fact, he didn't. This was a lesson in healing I wouldn't forget.

Chapter 37

Religion that God our Father accepts as pure and fault-
less is this: to look after orphans and widows in their
distress and to keep oneself from being polluted by the
world.

—James 1:27

Danai and I seemed to work well together as we took
turns serving meals on our flight to Grand Cayman
and back. Most of our downtime was spent reading, until
near the end of our final flight. "Are you Catholic?" she
asked me out of thin air.

"No," I replied.

Danai said that she was Catholic and that she noticed
my ring with a cross on it. "My mother thinks I'm turning
atheist," she said, laughing.

"Why is that?"

"Because I don't go to church much." Danai explained
that her low seniority prevented her from being off Sundays. She also said that she had a six-year-old son who was
autistic and that he made loud noises in church.

"It's important that you go," I said. "We all need that
kind of support." I assured Danai that her schedule would
improve with time, and I suggested that she attend a
church service on another night of the week.

Danai appreciated my suggestions and began to share
more about her struggles as a single mother. She said that
she was divorced, that she had no family living nearby,
and that she was halfway through an education program

at University of North Carolina. "I figure I can teach any-where if I need to," she added.

"Who watches your son?" I asked.

"A religious woman. She takes him to church some-times."

Danai's situation melted my heart. I knew what it was like to be divorced and to struggle through the initial five years of low pay as a stewardess. I couldn't imagine those circumstances being complicated further.

As she and I gathered our things upon landing, I be-gan to share that God had given her and me this divine appointment. Danai stopped in the aisle and turned and looked dead at me.

When we got off the airplane onto the Jetway, Danai and I were alone together. The rest of the crew had gone ahead to US Customs. "I feel so much compassion in my heart for you, Danai," I said. "It's the love of Jesus. He enables me to see people the way He sees them and love them the way He does."

Danai's eyes teared.

"He loves you so much," I said. "That's the message He wants me to give to you." I told Danai that Jesus wanted to encourage her and give her hope and blessings and that He waits for her to talk to Him. "He wants a relationship with you," I said. "Do you pray?"

Danai hesitated and then said nothing.

"Just talk to Him from your heart," I encouraged her. "Your prayers don't have to be structured or formal."

Soon, Danai and I rejoined the crew, cleared US Cus-toms, and walked down the concourse together. "God is developing me in intercessory prayer," I said.

"That's what my friend does," she replied. "The one who watches my son."

I felt the joy of the Lord course through my body. "God sent me to pray for you," I said. "That's how important you are to Him."

Danai's eyes teared again.

"I wish we had time to pray together," I said, "but the crew is waiting. I will pray for you as soon as I get into my hotel room."

Danai and I hugged each other right before she departed for her flight to Atlanta to pick up her son at her mother's home. "And go to church," I said with a smile.

"I pass a Presbyterian church on my way home," she said, "and there is a marquis out front that says, 'People who have dusty Bibles lead dirty lives.'"

Danai and I laughed.

As soon as I got into my hotel room in downtown Charlotte, I dropped to my knees and prayed for Danai. I asked the Lord to continue to send her strong Christians who could help lead her closer to Him and who could help share her daily burdens.

Chapter 38

But as for you, be strong and do not give up, for your work will be rewarded.

—2 Chronicles 15:7

On the third day of a trip, our Airbus 319 sat attached to a gate at the Kansas City airport with ninety-nine passengers on board. I was positioned in the rear galley when, suddenly, rain poured from a darkened sky. I peeked out portholes as high winds immediately and unexpectedly swirled around us, rocking the tail of our plane from side to side. When hail balls began to hit the plane's tin skin, I knew this wasn't a typical storm. I looked around and saw that the passengers seemed unmoved.

A few minutes later, I heard Peggy, the head stewardess, speak over the intercom: "Ladies and gentlemen, may I have your attention please. We will need all of you to deplane. Please leave all your belongings and deplane as quickly as possible." Passengers stood and slowly shuffled off the aircraft. A minute later, I heard Peggy's voice again, "Quickly," she said.

Once the last passenger deplaned, the captain stood at the head of the aisle and yelled back to me, "Tornado headed toward us! Hurry! Run!" I grabbed my laptop and tote and ran up the aisle and up the Jetway.

Once inside the terminal, we were quickly herded across the concourse and downstairs into the lower level. There, we huddled with our passengers. The captain walked up to me and explained that the air traffic control tower had been evacuated and someone had radioed our flight deck advising us to do the same.

A few minutes later, we were informed that the tornado had touched down across the tarmac from our airplane and that it had damaged the FedEx cargo center. I was sorry to hear about the FedEx building, but I was glad that I had anointed the airplane with oil and prayed over it when I initially boarded.

Within an hour after evacuating, we re-boarded the plane. Almost everyone returned, and most passengers seemed unmoved by what had occurred. My heart still raced a little as I stowed my bags back under the last row of seats. The sky had lightened, and the storm had passed over in a remarkable way. I knew in my heart that God would give me a rainbow. I searched out the porthole on the right side of the aircraft and waited, but I saw nothing. Then I looked out of the left porthole, and there they were: three of them in a row, arching up over the partly cloudy sky. One was vibrant, the others successively muted. I walked up the aisle to inform Peggy and the other steward, Juan. Peggy took a minute away from her busy first-class service to walk out onto the Jetway and peer through the window. The rainbows brought a smile to her face.

We took off about two hours late. Even at 33,000 feet of altitude, the turbulence wouldn't allow us to serve passengers. About halfway to Pittsburgh, a woman approached me and asked how much flight time remained and whether I had any headache medicine. She also said that she was on the verge of a panic attack and that she had forgotten to bring her medication.

I popped up from my jump seat and asked her to be seated, assuring her that I would bring her some headache medicine. She smiled and returned to her seat. I recalled seeing this woman in the Kansas City airport, and, at that time, I noticed that she was the only adult in our group who was traveling with children.

I notified Juan of the woman's condition and asked him to stand by with oxygen. "I'm going to kneel in the aisle and pray with her," I said.

Juan stood up and ripped the headrest off of my jump seat. Then he tossed it onto the aisle beside my knees. "Here," he said. "Kneel on this."

My heart melted as this muscled, former Miami-vice cop extended his compassion to us.

With the padding beneath my knees, I held onto the woman's armrest and asked her for her name.

"Nicole," she said.

I noticed that neither Nicole nor her young son had their seat belts fastened, and I asked her to do so. Then I handed her the medicine and put my arm around her back. "Do you believe in God?" I asked.

A big smile beamed across Nicole's face. "Yes," she replied. "In fact, I've been sitting here the entire flight, praying in tongues. I even called my mama and asked her to pray for me."

Nicole and I chuckled. She explained that she and her kids were a military family moving to Germany.

I assured her that everything was going to be all right and that I was a Christian. I explained to her that I had anointed the very airplane in which she sat, putting crosses over each door, and claiming the plane for Jesus Christ.

Nicole reached for my hands.

"God is not going to take us down on this flight," I said. "He's got me working on a project right now, and He's not finished with me yet." I told Nicole that I would like to pray for her, and she accepted enthusiastically. I held her hands tighter, and I pled the blood of Jesus over her. I rebuked Satan and his plans against Nicole, and I rebuked the spirit of anxiety. I asked God to send angels to surround and protect Nicole, and I asked God to be a firewall of protection around her.

Nicole reached out to me and hugged me. Her face was exuberant.

God wanted Nicole to know that He was going to take care of her all the way, and He used me—someone who used to struggle with panic attacks—to facilitate. Oh, how blessed I felt that God was using the challenges of my past to help others.

By the time we reached Pittsburgh, we were about two hours late. When we arrived, we learned that the final flight of our trip to Philadelphia had already departed. Crew scheduling had assigned another crew to work the flight. So there we were in Pittsburgh, along with a plane-load of passengers. We were informed that the hotels were full and that we had reservations at a local Motel 6. This was not a chain at which we normally stayed. Nonetheless, we were grateful to receive an additional five hours of pay for simply spending the night and riding back to Philadelphia early the next morning. I knew that God was in control, that He was faithful, and that He had just blessed us with a reward of extra rest and extra pay.

Chapter 39

Therefore encourage one another and build each other up, just as in fact you are doing.
— 1 Thessalonians 5:11

Driving from my home to the Philadelphia airport one Monday afternoon, God spoke to me. "I'm taking off the training wheels," He said. God assured me that He had trained me well on how to spot a divine appointment and what to do with one.

When I checked in for my trip on the crew lounge computer, I saw a familiar name pop up: Mattie. Instantly, I sensed that the divine appointment would be with her. Mattie and I had flown together years earlier in Washington, DC, long before I had begun to share God at my workplace. She was a single mother of a little girl named Sedona.

Our trip began, and Mattie and I greeted each other with a hug. Since we had never discussed God, I had no idea what Mattie's beliefs were.

As our trip progressed, we caught up on the circumstances of our lives. Sedona was almost a six-year-old now, and the two of them were planning to move out of their Washington, DC area apartment and back home with family in Ohio. Mattie explained that her apartment had recently gone on the market at a price she couldn't afford. She said that if she had received adequate child support from Sedona's father, Don, she may have been able to afford to buy her apartment a year earlier. But the only child support she received from him was to cover the cost of childcare when she worked trips.

I was a bit shocked to hear all of this. I was aware that Mattie had a contract with Don concerning Sedona and that she had decided to birth Sedona and raised her alone from the outset. I also understood that being a mother to Sedona without much assistance from Don was a challenge. My impression had always been that Mattie was happy about having a baby on her own and that she didn't desire Don's active role in Sedona's life at all.

But now, Mattie confessed to me how bittersweet Sedona's birth was. She explained that although her heart was filled with love, she felt attacked by Don and his father in the early days of Sedona's life. She felt threatened that they would try to take Sedona away from her if she did not agree to what would prove to be an inadequate amount of child support. She said that she had received many accolades from coworkers and friends for having chosen to have a baby on her own. But then she soon realized she loved Sedona so much that she wanted to give her everything, including a father. For years, Mattie had looked at Don to fill this desire. But she was consistently disappointed to witness Don dating other women and spending little time with Sedona.

Mattie said that now God was changing her circumstances, giving her a new direction, steering her path away from such false hope. He was leading her toward greater stability and support. She said that she and Sedona had been attending church and that Sedona loved the Lord. I felt blessed to hear this news, and I could hardly wait to pray with her.

For the next three days, Mattie and I shared our beliefs and our personal relationship with Christ. Through our conversations and prayers, I realized how much God had grown us in such a short time.

$$\mathscr{Chapter}\ 40$$

A man's wisdom gives him patience; it is to his glory to overlook an offense.

—Proverbs 19:11

God had trained me well. With my first impression of Anne, I sensed the divine appointment would be with her. Our trip began early on a Monday morning, and I hadn't had much sleep. When I boarded our aircraft, Anne informed me that she would like to work in the rear of the aircraft and offered me the first-class position. Since I had prayed for God to choose a position for me, I declined, saying I would like to keep my coach position. Anne replied that she was senior to me and that she was taking my position. I figured God had a purpose in this, and besides, I had no choice. So I smiled and chose to not walk in offense.

I was very quiet during the first day of our trip, not because I was angry but because I was physically exhausted. As I witnessed Anne's interaction with me grow defensive and bitter, it became clear to me that she interpreted my quietness as despondence directed toward her. I knew that she had no reason to be angry with me and that whatever was pulling her down was likely a personal issue. Anne made a passing comment which indicated that she and her husband were having problems. As the day progressed, I noticed that any little thing would easily affect her temperament in a negative way.

On the second day of our trip, my energy level was higher. Even our captain noticed and commented that I was "alive." When Anne realized that my initial quietness had nothing to do with her, she responded in a friendlier manner toward me. She and I shared conversation involving divorce and stepchildren. She then shared that her husband was going to meet her on our Atlanta layover. She said that he had taken a new job there but she was not ready to join him and move from their house in Delaware.

On the third and final day of our trip, I walked to the back of the aircraft and sat on an armrest of a passenger seat to talk with Anne. As we spoke, Anne warmed up even more and began to share further about herself and her troubled marriage. She said she had been married for ten years and that she and her husband had received pastoral counseling. She said her husband had done something very "dark," and, as a result of his behavior, she had been treating him differently. She said she had been trying to forgive him and move beyond the incident but she still struggled.

"I'd like to share a secret with you," I said. I explained that I had prayed for God to choose a trip for me and to choose each crew member on the trip. "He chose you," I said.

Anne's eyes immediately filled with tears. "I had a feeling about this," she said.

I explained to her that God gives me divine appointments on each trip. "This time it's with you," I said.

Anne cried. She opened up to me, telling me that she had been doing everything she knew to overcome her obstacles. She said that she had grown closer to the Lord through the incident with her husband. "My husband was a big Christian when I married him," she said. "That's one of the reasons I married him." Anne said that there was a particular person who led him into darkness. She explained that if he hadn't been so remorseful over the incident, she didn't think she would still be married to him.

God enabled me to see Anne's heart, and I could tell that she loved her husband and wanted their marriage to work. "God has called me to pray for you," I said. "And besides, I need the practice."

As we walked to the rear galley, I understood why Anne wanted to work in the back of the airplane. Working in the front, which was often chaotic and full of enplaning and deplaning passengers, would have been too much for her.

We sat on the rear jump seat, and I anointed her with oil. Then I held her hands and prayed. I prayed warfare prayers over Anne and her husband, Alan, and I asked God for the restoration of her marriage and for many other blessings. When we finished, Anne and I embraced.

Anne then mentioned that she was scheduled to fly a two-day trip the following day. I said that I needed to pick up a two-day trip, and she asked me to fly hers. I smiled and reminded her that I ask God to choose the trips and the crew.

The following day, I reported for the two-day trip that God had chosen for me. It was the one on which Anne was scheduled. When I arrived at the aircraft, Anne wasn't there. She had been replaced by a stewardess junior to her, who had been on call. When I inquired about the situation, the stewardess informed me that Anne had shown up for the trip without her airline ID and was sent home. I sensed that God would give this replacement stewardess and me a divine appointment.

Chapter 41

"Therefore go and make disciples of all nations, baptizing them in the name of the Father and of the Son and of the Holy Spirit, and teaching them to obey everything I have commanded you . . ."

—Matthew 28:19-20

Even from the beginning of our three-day trip, Gene read his Bible. "I see you're a Christian," I said to him. "I am too."

Gene smiled.

I shared with him that I had prayed before our trip and asked God to handpick each crew member.

Gene seemed a little surprised. He thought for a minute and said that would explain why he had been assigned this trip from crew scheduling when it was not included in a list of trip choices he had submitted to them.

This news tickled me because it was another confirmation that crew scheduling was not in control of our working lives but rather the omnipotent God.

Gene went on to say that he had requested only four-day trips and that, with his seniority, he should have, by all human logic, received one of them. But God had higher plans. God wanted Gene on this trip, just like He wanted me, and Sabrina, too.

Gene pulled out a business card from his wallet and handed it to me. It read, "JesusNOW Ministries, Gene Kelley, President/Senior Minister." Gene shared that he had an evangelical ministry in Montreal and that his wife was also a stewardess for our airline. I was awed that God had chosen a minister to pair me with on this trip, and I sensed that He had something big in store for us.

God placed me in the coach cabin to work with Sabrina. Half-empty airplanes allowed Sabrina and me time to sit in the last row of coach seats and chat. I recalled Sabrina's pretty face from having worked with her years earlier in Washington, DC. As Sabrina and I caught up, I noticed that she seemed tense. Many of her words were either critical or complaining in nature, and most of the topics she chose to bring up seemed petty. I got the impression that everything agitated and disappointed her.

For three full months now, I had witnessed bad attitudes of epidemic proportions among stewardesses. And each time I had flown with them, Jesus showed His face. Every time. Therefore, I believed that He was on to something and that He would surface in Sabrina's case.

On our second day of flying, our crew had a long break in the Philadelphia airport. Sabrina and I agreed to have lunch together. She shared with me that she had been divorced for two years. As a result, she had ceased attending her Catholic church, and she took to flying on Sundays. She filled me in on the details saying that she was living in an expensive apartment in Center City, that she still was on her ex-husband's expensive auto insurance policy, and was loosely tied to a boyfriend whom she had had since her separation. Sabrina didn't know where to move to start a new life. She considered returning to Washington, DC, but she admitted to not having peace about any options. Toward the end of our conversation, Sabrina's eyes filled with tears. "I feel hopeless," she said.

That was all I needed to hear. I took a deep breath, and I began to witness to her. I said that I understood she needed guidance in her life.

"Yes!" she exclaimed, "That's it! That's what I need!"

I knew her words were a sign of encouragement from God, and so I continued, "You know, Jesus can give you that if you invite Him into your heart."

Sabrina's face brightened at this opportunity of hope.

I laughed big and shared with Sabrina that God had sent Gene and me to help her with this.

"Really?!" Sabrina shouted.

I informed her that Gene was a minister and that God loved her so much that He sent a minister and a sister in Christ to her. Then I quoted Jeremiah 29:11-13, which promises that God has a plan for her.

Sabrina was ecstatic. Her face beamed with her biggest smile yet.

For me, this was an amazing blessing and breakthrough because I had never actually led anyone to fully accept the Lord as Savior before. God broke through my fear and provided a way. I knew that the opposite of fear was love, and I knew that Sabrina could see the love of Jesus in me because she said so. God had, indeed, brought me far.

I explained to Sabrina what being born again meant. I explained the salvation prayer, how inviting Jesus into her heart was different from learning doctrine. I offered to lay hands on her and pray for her during our next flight. Then I asked her for her permission to reveal all of this to Gene and invite him to pray for her as well.

Sabrina enthusiastically embraced my offer.

Once on the airplane, I barely had time to share the good news with Gene before passengers boarded. So I shared the news with him in the forward galley while he poured drinks for first class.

Gene was ecstatic. He saw the situation as miraculous. He peeked around the galley corner, down the aisle, peering at Sabrina. She smiled big and waved. Gene rehashed how he had gotten this trip in the first place, that it was not one he had chosen. He understood that it was chosen for him by God for His purpose of saving a soul.

Once in flight, Sabrina and I served the coach cabin while Gene served first class. All the while, I felt a sense of urgency to pray for Sabrina. Like a runner in the starting blocks, I was ready.

In little time, Gene, Sabrina, and I huddled in the last row of passenger seats. Gene began by sharing with Sabrina how he had gotten this trip. Sabrina laughed and shared that she had picked this trip up by an unlikely choice, that it touched a two-day trip she had just gotten in from the night before, and that she never flies two trips back to back.

Gene explained the process of salvation to Sabrina, how she would be a child of God, how her life would change, how she would need to change her priorities and put God first in all aspects of her life, and how she would have an eternal place reserved in heaven. Gene also offered her information on a church in downtown Philadelphia where she lived: Living Word Community Church. Gene explained that he had met the pastor on a flight years earlier.

Sabrina gasped when she saw the church's address. It was only ten blocks from her apartment. She said that she was ready, and I began by laying my hands on her and praying. Sabrina wept. I put my arm around her and held her as I continued to pray.

When Gene took over, Sabrina cried even more. I sat and marveled at how God used Gene to explain the meaning of God's salvation to a humbled Sabrina. He knelt beside her as she sat on the jump seat, and he led her gently in the salvation prayer.

I felt so blessed to have been chosen to help lead a soul to God. It humbled my heart enormously. Through this, I felt strengthened to lead others to Christ. Through this, my faith and trust were deepened that God, indeed, reached the seemingly unreachable, which, in this case, was a coworker that He placed right in my path.

Three months later, almost to the day, God paired me with Sabrina on another trip. This time, He blessed us with an Aruba layover. Sabrina and I rested on the beach and caught up. Then we met up with Lee Ann, the other Christian stewardess with whom we worked, and had dinner. God provided us with a lovely atmosphere in which to share and encourage one another.

Three more months later, I crossed paths with Sabrina again in the Philadelphia airport. We greeted each other with a hug, and she informed me that she had moved out of the city, bought a condo in the suburbs, and begun attending church. Praise the Lord!

Chapter 42

Praise be to the God and Father of our Lord Jesus Christ, the Father of compassion and the God of all comfort, who comforts us in all our troubles, so that we can comfort those in any trouble with the comfort we ourselves have received from God.

—2 Corinthians 1:3-4

I knew something very special had to happen on this trip, because God chose one for me that departed early on a type of aircraft that I did not usually fly.

As my alarm clock went off at 2:30 a.m., I tried not to loath getting up. I thanked God for the trip and asked Him to enable me to see what He wanted me to see. I asked Him to make me the disciple He wanted me to be. Then I lay in bed for fifteen minutes before rising.

I packed all of my last-minute toiletries into my suitcase. Then I picked up the plastic case of Dr. Charles Stanley's *Growing Strong In Faith* tapes that I had found in a box the evening prior. Listening to Dr. Stanley's voice always comforts me, and, in this case, it also helped me to stay awake on my two-hour commute.

I arrived in the Philadelphia crew lounge several minutes before check-in, which was 6 a.m. I signed in for my trip on one of the many computer terminals and then retrieved the company mail out of my box. I plopped on a sofa against a wall to read my mail, my eyes barely able to remain open. And then I heard a man's voice. I looked up to see a captain I knew well. His name was Mark.

"We're flying together," Mark said with a Cheshire-cat smile.

Stunned, I just sat and stared at him. Then slowly and silently, I asked God, "What is this?"

"Don't sit there like you don't know me," Mark said.

I was so fatigued when I checked in for the trip that, even though I looked at the names of the other crew members on the list, I didn't see Mark's. And now, I was assigned to fly with a former friend, one from my carnal Christian days.

Finally, I stood and walked over to Mark. "I didn't know we were flying together," I said. "I'm a 'Jesus freak' now, you know."

Mark laughed. "'Jesus freak'?" he replied.

"Yeah." Mark and I chatted for a while before meeting up later at our aircraft.

Once there, I met Jennifer, our head stewardess. I was assigned to be the stewardess who floated between first class and coach. This was fine with me because our Airbus 319 was fairly new to me, and I had much to learn. Mark led our crew briefing, and then we dispersed to set up the cabin for passengers. I asked for God to place angels inside and outside the airplane. Then I walked out onto the Jetway and placed a big oily cross aside the aircraft door threshold. Now, we were ready.

On they came. Jennifer and I nodded and smiled and greeted. We hung coats, suit jackets, poured coffee, and served orange juice. While in the galley together, she turned to me and asked, "So how did you get this trip?"

I knew what she meant. She didn't understand why someone with my seniority would choose to fly such a difficult, early trip. I decided to be bold and replied, "I just prayed and asked God to pick one for me, and He chose this one."

Jennifer smiled wide with a little giggle.

After flying three legs together, we were scheduled to sit in the Charlotte airport for about an hour. During this hour, Mark and I decided to sit together and chat over Krispy Kreme donuts and a Cinnabon roll, old favorites of ours. Mark and I first met in 1994 while based in Washington, DC, when he was a captain on the DC-9, and I had just begun graduate school at New York University. Our dating relationship lasted for a year and a half. As we talked and laughed, there was absolutely no temptation for me to fall back into this relationship. In fact, God had grown me to see Mark in a whole new way: sad and lonely. Mark asked me how my writing was going, and I shared with him that God had called me to write this book. I explained how God chooses trips for me and then gives me divine appointments on them. Mark laughed.

On the second day of our trip, we flew three legs, including Grand Cayman to Charlotte. Mark and I were the last two crew members to clear US Customs. We found ourselves walking side by side up the concourse to our next flight. Just a few steps in front of us, I spotted coins on the floor. "Pennies!" I exclaimed. "They're back!" Mark looked at me like I was a nut. I knelt down to pick up each of them. There were seven, plus one dime. "It's a sign," I said.

"A sign of what?" he asked.

"It's encouragement from God. Something big is about to happen. Most of the time He gives me only one or two, but there are seven. That means whatever is about to happen is really special."

Mark laughed and told me that he threw those pennies on the floor for me to find.

"You need Jesus," I replied.

That afternoon, as we checked into our Charlotte hotel, Jennifer commented to our copilot about him being left-handed. Mark spoke up and said that he also used to be left-handed, but that the nuns "beat it out of him" when he was very young. Then he mentioned that they didn't teach phonics back then either, that he was taught to read by rote (memory). I had forgotten that Mark had been raised Catholic.

On the third and final day of our trip, I worked in the first-class galley preparing hot lunches for a few passengers traveling from Montego Bay to Charlotte. We switched to an Airbus 321, which is considerably longer than our former 319 and, therefore, requires that two stewardesses work in first class. I made drinks and cooked and plated food in the forward galley while Jennifer served the passengers. We were a team. Working together in such a close, intimate space offers its challenges and its blessings.

At one point, Jennifer turned to me and said that she was considering moving into her own apartment in Center City, Philadelphia, and that she was seeking a church. This didn't surprise me at all because one of the things I had learned about letting others know that I am Christian is that they often see an open door to share their soul. I said to Jennifer that I had the name of a church and its pastor in Center City and that I had received it from a steward who was also an ordained minister. Jennifer said she would love to have the information, and so I passed it on to her.

Jennifer then asked me why Mark and I broke up. I explained that Mark and I weren't very compatible.

"People are brought to us for a season sometimes," she said compassionately.

"Yes," I replied, "but I shouldn't have gotten so involved with him. I should have turned to safer people." Jennifer smiled and nodded. I knew she was struggling with a "man issue" herself, even though she didn't elaborate much on it. Nonetheless, I hoped that my testimony would inspire her to make godly choices in this area.

After our service, I walked out into the aisle and spotted a familiar face in seat 7C. The man's name was Ken, and he was a gate agent in Pittsburgh. As I approached Ken, he reached for my hand and held it. "It's so nice to see my girls," he said, smiling.

"Likewise," I replied. "It's been so long. How are you?"

Ken said he was fine and that he was returning home from escorting his mother back to Jamaica. He explained that she had been very sick, that she had been in a coma while she was visiting him in the United States. Ken said God had healed his mother and that she was fine now.

"Is this your wife?" I asked Ken, looking at the woman seated beside him.

"No," he replied. "I just met this kind lady in the terminal, and she has Jesus all over her."

I extended my hand to the lady and introduced myself.

"My name is Tisha," she replied. Ken reached for my hand again and also for Tisha's. He said that he was a born-again Christian and he wanted to pray.

"I'm born again too," I said.

"Praise God," he replied. "I'm a missionary. That's my purpose."

Ken's words really spoke to me because I was so delightfully surprised to meet another coworker who regarded himself as such, who sought a higher purpose in his work and who knew that God had placed him in his job to accomplish His will. I had crossed paths with Ken many times while based in Pittsburgh in the early nineties. He always had a smile on his face. Though I didn't know him well, there was something about him that always seemed to comfort me, like a father's heart, and I enjoyed being in his presence. Now I knew why.

The three of us closed our eyes, and Ken led us in a brief prayer of praise and thanksgiving.

I asked Tisha whether she was an agent too, and she said that she worked in the corporate offices. Ken mentioned that Tisha was overcoming a painful breakup with a man. I looked into Tisha's eyes, and I could see her anguish. I didn't ask her why she was in Jamaica. I simply said, "I would be happy to pray for you."

Tisha seemed pleased at this offer, and I felt led to loan her one of my Christian books to read during the flight. Then I went into the lavatory to pray for Tisha. Since the front row of first class was empty, I sat in a window seat on the opposite side of the aircraft from Tisha to finish reading a spiritual warfare book. The Holy Spirit illuminated the author's concept of healing to me, and then He put Tisha on my heart again. I prayed for her again. I continued to read, and, just moments later, I felt an urge to look out the window. When I did, I saw a rainbow. A parhelion appeared just above the second cloud layer, and I knew it was a confirmation that the Lord was healing Tisha's heart.

I walked back to Tisha, who was quietly reading, and I shared with her that God had just presented a rainbow. Tears immediately fell from Tisha's cheeks. "It's a sign that it's going to be OK," she said.

I reached for Tisha's hands. They were soft and warm. I rubbed them and said, "God bless you, sister. Praise God."

"Yes," Tisha replied.

There was a couple sitting in the row in front of Tisha, and I knew they could overhear our conversation. I also knew God planted them there to do just that. He was working all around us, and I was reveling in His presence.

Tisha shared with me that she had lowered herself in her relationship with the man she had just broken up with, and she felt worn out.

"God has something better in mind for you," I affirmed to her. "He loves you very much. He wants what's best for you."

Tisha cried harder. "I know," she replied. "I'm enjoying this book." It was *The Prayer of Jabez*.

I knew as I left her presence that God had chosen me to deliver this message because He knew that He had used my former pain to transform my heart into a compassionate one. I returned to my seat, barely able to sit still because I was so thrilled to do God's work. I lived for such moments.

After we landed, Tisha returned my book to me and thanked me again. "God bless you," I replied.

As passengers filed off the aircraft, two young men wearing Jesus T-shirts approached me. I smiled big, gave them a thumbs-up, and blurted out, "All right! Praise God!" I was amazed at how bold the Lord had grown me.

After everyone deplaned, our crew gathered our belongings and headed to US Customs. En route, Mark walked beside me. "A miracle happened on this flight," I said to him.

Mark smiled.

"God showed me a rainbow."

Mark laughed. "Rainbow?" he said with disdain. "Tell me about it."

"Nah. You wouldn't get it."

When we boarded our Airbus 319 again, it was the final leg of our trip. This time, I not only anointed the airplane's doors, I anointed the captain's seat. I put a cross on the back of the seat that Mark would sit in for the next hour and a half and claimed it for Jesus.

During our descent, Jennifer and I were strapped into our jump seats, which brought us nose to nose with each other once again. "It's funny," she said, "I don't think I've ever flown a trip where a crew didn't complain about their jobs until this one."

I giggled inside because I knew God's presence and peace abounded. Jennifer had witnessed me putting crosses above the doors at least once. I had tried to be discreet and do it when no one was around, but sometimes there wasn't time to be discreet. She never mentioned anything about it, but I knew that she knew the presence of God was with us. And I'm certain that it made an impression on her.

Once in our home base of Philadelphia, we bid each other farewell, and Mark and I walked out to the crew bus stop together. "So why do you think God brought us together?" I asked him.

Mark lit up a cigarette and took a puff. "To torture us?" he said, laughing.

I just shook my head and laughed. And then I prayed for him on my drive home.

Chapter 43

He himself bore our sins in his body on the tree, so that we might die to sins and live for righteousness; by his wounds you have been healed.

—1 Peter 2:24

Marie was an extraordinarily beautiful young woman. She was tall and slender with raven hair pulled straight back in a smooth chignon. Her eyebrows were perfectly arched over her soft brown eyes. And her sweet personality made her a joy to fly with.

At the outset of our trip, Marie commented that she was a bit preoccupied with concerns of her five-year-old nephew, Ned. She said that he was due to come home from the hospital in a few days.

As passengers poured on board for our first flight, Marie informed me that two weeks earlier, she and her family had learned that Ned was diagnosed with aplastic anemia, a condition that inhibits the bone marrow's healthy production of blood cells and platelets.

Almost immediately, I excused myself and locked myself in the lavatory and prayed for Ned.

Over the course of our first day of flying five legs together, Marie shared more details about Ned's situation. She said that he was in the hospital receiving blood transfusions and other treatments and, with this prescribed plan of attack, he had a seventy to eighty percent chance of survival, according to his doctors.

Marie was very close to Ned, as she lived with him and his family. Her face brightened when she spoke of how she had looked forward to coming home off her trips to find Ned waiting for her. "Now," she said, "it's not the same."

I asked Marie if I could pray for her. She consented, and I took her hands and thanked God for this divine appointment and His healing mercy. As Marie cried, I beseeched God on behalf of her family to heal Ned. When we finished, Marie hugged me and said she felt better. The Holy Spirit enlightened me that, through me, God offered Marie the loving hope of Jesus.

"I must've been meant to fly with you," Marie said.

"I have a secret," I replied, laughing. "We were most definitely meant to fly together." I explained to Marie that I pray for divine appointments before every trip, even for God to choose a trip for me.

"That makes sense," Marie said, "because I wasn't supposed to be on this trip. Crew scheduling just called me this morning for it."

"God is the sovereign scheduler," I said, chuckling.

Marie and I shared a laugh, and she opened up even more, saying that she was beginning to feel like she couldn't handle life any longer, that her sister, Ned's mother, was also separated from Ned's father and that her aunt also had cancer.

I knew we had a lot more praying to do.

Marie also shared that on her previous trip she felt death surround her. She said that the copilot's father had just been removed from his respirator, that a boyfriend of one of the stewardesses was dying, and that another stewardess had a relative who was dying. "They kept talking about death on the hotel van," Marie said. "I finally got to my room and cried."

"No wonder God picked you for this trip," I replied. "He knew that you really needed to hear from Him."

"Sometimes I get so down," Marie said. "The little boy who was in Ned's hospital room right before him died." Marie explained that she was still trying to make sense of everything and that all this had happened only two weeks ago.

I explained to Marie that God had anointed me for healing and He was teaching me how to pray for people to receive their healing. "You and Ned are such blessings to me," I said, "because, even in the midst of this trial, God is present, and He is moving on your behalf." I retrieved *Healing Prayer* from my tote and showed it to Marie, saying, "It's no accident that I have this book with me."

Marie, once again, acknowledged that we were meant to fly together and that her family wasn't very spiritual. She said they were Catholic and they attended Mass, but that was about it.

I explained to Marie that God would use Ned's illness to bring her family closer to Him.

Marie looked pensive and admitted that everyone in her immediate family had been praying together. She said her mother had gotten out her rosary beads in Ned's hospital room, where she prayed relentlessly.

I explained to Marie the importance of having a personal relationship with God, about knowing Him, growing in Him, doing the work of Jesus, and leaning upon Him in times of despair and joy. "It's like having a close friend," I said. "If we don't keep in touch and nurture the friendship, we grow distant." I explained that God is our Father and, that as such, He loves us unendingly and waits for our return to Him.

Marie listened intently.

"It's about fully inviting Jesus into our hearts," I said, "and living a life according to His will."

Marie suddenly gasped. "I just remembered something," she said. "Ned has been talking about Jesus being a 'lifesaver.'" Marie explained that Ned talked about a riddle, asking how many lifesavers Jesus had. Then Ned would announce, "One." "I don't know where he got that from," Marie said, "because no one in my family talks about Jesus like that." Marie said when she asked Ned where he learned the riddle he said he didn't know but that he just knew it.

"Sounds like the Holy Spirit," I said. "God is speaking to that child, and He is speaking to you and your family through that child." I explained to Marie that all children belong to Jesus and that parents and aunts and siblings just get to borrow children for a while. "Everything we think we own really belongs to God."

Marie nodded and tried to understand. "Nothing like this has ever happened to our family," she replied.

As I flipped through *Healing Prayer*, I felt led to share a couple of sections that would bring comfort to Marie. I showed them to her and then handed the book to her and suggested that she read it on our long layover in Syracuse.

Once we got into our rooms, I wrote Marie and her family's names in my prayer journal so I could continue to pray for them as I had promised Marie I would do. I knew they were my assignment.

The next day, on our layover, I readied myself and headed downstairs to locate a church. Just one block away was the beautiful Cathedral of the Immaculate Conception, on East Onondaga Street. From the moment I entered the sanctuary, I could hardly wait to pray. I lowered the kneeling bench and got on my knees and beseeched God on Ned's behalf once again.

When I finished, I returned to my room and telephoned Marie to tell her about the church. But there was no answer.

A little later, I met the crew downstairs in the lobby for a day of flying. There was Marie, sitting in an elegant, antique wingback chair. We greeted each other casually, and then Marie stepped closer to me. "I slept so well last night," she said, "better than I had in a long time."

"Praise God," I said. "Before I went to bed last night, I prayed that God would give you a good night's sleep, as if you had been sleeping for three days."

Marie was so delighted. I knew that God was encouraging me to keep praying and that this was a testament that God had heard her needs and was bringing her to a more intimate relationship with Him.

Exactly one month later to the day, I crossed paths with Marie on the stair landing of the crew lounge. I was so delighted to see her. I asked her about Ned and she said his condition had improved. I assured her I would continue to pray for him.

Chapter 44

"If you believe, you will receive whatever you ask for in prayer."

—Matthew 21:22

I awoke on September 11, 2002, to a message from my friend, Donna, saying that she was thinking of me. Donna and I had flown together the day before the previous year's bombings, and she felt comfort in reaching out to me on this memorable day. I was blessed.

I began flying a trip on September 10th, just like Donna's and my trip last year. I had asked God to provide me with an easy time and for an endearing divine appointment. The light loads afforded Stephanie, Pam, and me to sit in the rear of our Boeing 737 and share testimony and prayer. We were blessed.

Stephanie immediately shared that she was self-conscious of her south Philadelphia accent and that the international stewardesses teased her. She also shared that she struggled with reflex sympathetic dystrophy (RSD), a neurological syndrome. Stephanie had been raised Catholic and now attended a Charismatic Catholic church. She said that through prayer at her church, God had freed her body of this affliction.

Pam, on the other hand, was at risk of being furloughed from our airline in their attempt to streamline costs and recover from bankruptcy. She had only a few years of seniority.

"Do you believe in God?" I asked her.

"Yes," she replied, smiling. Pam added that she had recently accepted Jesus.

I felt joy fill my heart, and I shared Jeremiah 29:11-13 with Pam. The Holy Spirit had led me to deliver this scripture many times before to coworkers who faced furlough or seemingly uncertain futures.

As Pam read the verses, a smile graced her face and her eyes brightened. "I feel like crying," she said. Pam explained that she had just found a tiny New Testament Bible in a compartment in the rear galley. She confessed that she was, in her words, "living in sin" with her boyfriend and that he, in fact, had led her to the Lord but that they were currently not attending church. Concerning her career, she said that she was planning to move back to her hometown in Pennsylvania and return to college to earn a degree in nursing.

As Pam spoke, I felt an overwhelming desire to pray for these two women. So that evening, in the back of the airplane, the three of us sat in a row of passenger seats and held hands. I anointed both Stephanie and Pam and allowed the Spirit to lead me in prayer. Tears streamed down Stephanie's face as we prayed. Pam said she had never participated in this type of laying-on of hands before, and she expressed that no one had ever done this for her. She said she felt like crying too.

Over the past two and a half days, Stephanie had relayed to me information about our copilot's future. I learned that he was about to be furloughed, too, and that he lacked one thousand hours of flight time to receive a type rating that could make him more valuable in the eyes of the airline industry for rehire. Stephanie commented repeatedly that she was so touched at his gentle attitude and demeanor. She felt compassion for him. And now, his situation had gotten to my heart too. So when he walked out of the flight deck on the last day of our trip, I said to Matt, "Do you believe in God?"

"Yes," he replied.

"We want to pray for you," I said.

Matt smiled and consented.

We three stewardesses circled around Matt in the back of the cabin and anointed him and prayed. I asked God for His provision and to draw Matt closer.

Later that evening, Pam expressed that she would like to get off the trip in Charlotte, just before our last leg home. She lived in Norfolk and hoped that another commuting stewardess would be kind enough to work for her on our last leg to Philadelphia. If no one was available, Pam would have to spend the night in Philadelphia and return to Norfolk the next morning. Stephanie immediately spoke up and declared that God would provide someone for her.

Sure enough, once we arrived in Charlotte, several commuting stewardesses waited to board our flight. Stephanie assisted Pam in locating one who would work for her. When I showed up at the gate, Pam approached me exuberantly. "It worked!" she said. "Someone is willing to work for me!"

During our final flight home, Stephanie informed me that Pam witnessed to the group of stewardesses who were available to fly for her, saying that we had prayed for her to go home early and that God had blessed her.

Chapter 45

"His master replied, 'Well done, good and faithful servant! You have been faithful with a few things; I will put you in charge of many things. Come and share your master's happiness!'"

—Matthew 25:21

Kate and I had flown together years ago, before I had begun sharing God's love at work. While flying this first trip together, an incident occurred that left us feeling at odds with each other.

Several years passed. Then, one day while scanning the crew lounge bulletin board, I spotted a memo concerning Kate. The memo had been posted for the purpose of informing coworkers that Kate was battling cancer. As I stood and prayed for Kate, the Holy Spirit convicted me that I still carried bitterness toward her over the incident that occurred years earlier. So I stopped praying for Kate, and I confessed my sin.

A few more years passed, and God paired me with Kate again. Over the course of flying this trip, I watched Kate retrieve medication from her tote. She showed me snapshots of herself recovering from radiation and chemotherapy. And then she pulled back her collar and showed me her neck, which had a concave shape on one side. She explained that she had to have a large artery removed from this area and that it still felt as though someone was clinching it. She said she also had had several lymph nodes removed and suffered with dry mouth as a result of treatments.

Her spirit seemed surprisingly up, and she didn't seem angry about her circumstances. This piqued my interest. I asked Kate about her spiritual walk, and she shared that she had been raised in the church and was a Christian. She said that her family and friends at her church prayed for her throughout her ordeal and that she believed in the power of prayer.

"I would like to pray for you too," I said.

Kate's face lit up.

On our final layover, I invited Kate into my room. We talked about walking in God's will and how Jesus came to heal the broken. Then I anointed her with oil and prayed over her body, soul, and spirit. When I finished, Kate opened her eyes and said she felt tingling from the top of her head to the tips of her toes. I believe this to have been a manifestation of the Holy Spirit. Kate and I stood and hugged and rejoiced in celebration of God's power and blessings.

For the first nine hours of the following day, Kate did not have to take the medicine that added moisture to her mouth. And the tightness in her neck had been mostly relieved. I felt humbled and encouraged at the partial healing God had done, and I stood believing that He would do a complete work.

Toward the end of our day, Kate turned to me on the jump seat with an idea: to pray over the notices posted on the crew lounge bulletin board, the ones that listed other stewardesses who battled critical illnesses or who had lost loved ones.

I was delighted that she reminded me to do this. And so I committed myself to praying for these people each week when I checked in for my trips.

I walked off our second trip feeling jubilant, knowing that if I had continued to harbor ill feelings toward Kate for an incident that had occurred years earlier, I would not have been able to do the work of Jesus.

Weeks later, I found myself in the Pittsburgh International airport with a few free hours to spend in between flights. I got something to eat and went upstairs to sit in an area that was unoccupied. This was an area that I had not ventured to in years, one where I used to sit and pray in silence after our airline's crashes. I noticed that the area had changed and that an airport chapel had been added.

When I finished eating, I entered the chapel and sat down in the quiet and prayed. Then I walked to the front of the room and spotted a journal lying on the pulpit. I opened it and began to read the entries. Many of them were written on or after September 11, 2001. I was particularly touched by one woman's words. She was a Christian and had lost her husband to lung cancer. His name was the same as my uncle's who also had died of lung cancer. The Holy Spirit brought to mind what Kate had suggested: to pray over people whose names were posted on the bulletin boards. I received a revelation that this chapel journal was a kind of bulletin board. My heart melted, and I began to weep. Then I prayed over each person. I knew when I walked out of there that God had answered my Jabez prayer, that He was truly expanding my territory of prayer intercession.

Chapter 46

"But I tell you: Love your enemies and pray for those who persecute you . . ."

—Matthew 5:44

I had known Fran for eighteen years. We had worked together as gate agents when we first began our airline careers, many years before either of us worked as stewardesses. Over time, Fran and I had crossed paths in airports in various cities. At one point, we were even neighbors in Pittsburgh. And now, God had brought us together once more. I knew His favor was upon me when I saw Fran's name listed on our trip.

Our first day required a 2 a.m. wake-up for me. By the time I had commuted nearly two hours to work and boarded our Boeing 757, I was barely able to stand. Fran wanted to chat right away, but I simply was not capable. I apologized to her and to God for being so despondent, and I asked God to carry me through the morning.

After our first flight to Orlando, Fran and I found a couple of not-so-private seats in a gate area. We had a few hours to pass before our next flight, and we had a lot of catching up to do.

Fran was overwrought with issues concerning her marriage. She explained that her husband had had an adulterous affair months earlier and that she and her husband were seeking a new counselor. As God would have it, I happened to have my premarital counselor's business card in my wallet. I handed it to Fran. Then we pulled out our Bibles.

As we shared scripture, several airline workers stopped to chat with Fran. They knew her because she lived in Orlando and commuted weekly to our crew base in Philadelphia. I believe that God used us, even then, to plant seeds in these people as they noticed our open Bibles in our laps.

After working our next two flights, we were exhausted. As I climbed into my hotel bed, I opened my Bible and began to skim through some of my favorite passages. I asked the Holy Spirit to illuminate ones of restoration that I could share with Fran the following day.

The next morning, God blessed our crew with an easy day of only one flight back to our base. After our beverage service, I walked to the rear of our Boeing 757, where it was completely devoid of passengers. Pure luxury—this section was my favorite—because sitting back there alone enabled me to feel like I was on a private jet. Only this time, I was seated with Fran beside me in the early morning darkness.

Fran and I held hands and prayed. Although I had prayed so many times for other stewardesses, this one was extra special to my heart. Fran was a familiar soul, yet we had never shared much about the heart of Jesus. Now, after all these years, God had brought us together for this very purpose. I handed Fran the scriptures that I had written on a hotel pad of paper earlier that morning. She agreed that she would read them, meditate on them, and pray them back to God. I assured Fran that God had heard her cries and that bringing us together for this purpose was His confirmation.

I explained that I had prayed for God to pick the trip we were on and for Him to choose every crew member. "He chose you," I said, smiling. "He heard your cries and wanted to give you breakthrough." Fran and I hugged and delighted in the Lord. We knew God had opened a big door of intimacy between us as well as a window of hope for her marriage.

What's more, God chose me—someone who Fran teased years earlier about having been divorced—to pray for her and her third marriage. Indeed, God had brought us far.

Chapter 47

"I tell you the truth, anyone who has faith in me will do what I have been doing. He will do even greater things than these, because I am going to the Father."

—John 14:12

One morning as I checked in for my trip, a stewardess approached me and asked me which trip I was assigned. Ironically, we were assigned the same trip. She then asked me whether I would be willing to switch trips with one of her friends, who, she presumed, wanted to fly with her. I replied that I believed God had chosen my assigned trip for me and that I was reluctant to switch. At that moment, her friend arrived and said she did not want to switch. "I'm so embarrassed," Amanda said to me. "I guess God really wants you to be on our trip."

Minutes later, we boarded our airplane. Amanda seemed awkward about her earlier request to switch trips with me and apologized. She also explained that she usually takes one-day trips, partly to avoid flying with stewardesses who have difficult personalities. I understood completely.

Both of us knew what it felt like to be unwelcome in a new crew base due to seniority issues. I mentioned how shortly after my transfer from Baltimore to Philadelphia, the Holy Spirit spoke to me, telling me to pray for God to choose trips for me and to choose every crew member on the trip. I explained to Amanda that God also changed me to respond to the Holy Spirit instead of reacting to difficult personalities. "If I did fly with one," I said, "I knew that God had chosen them for a purpose."

Amanda seemed to enjoy this testimony and felt relieved that I was a Christian. I learned that she was too.

After the cabin was boarded for our first flight, I turned to the floater steward, Lon, and struck up a conversation with him in the galley. I learned that he lived in Center City and knew all about the Philadelphia train system. I shared that I might be driving up for an event in the city, and I asked him which train line I should take. Lon was very kind in providing me with the information, and then he asked me about the event.

"It's a Christian conference," I said.

Lon commented that he had been raised Catholic, then converted to Pentecostal, became born again, and now did not believe in much organized religion. He said that he believed in a more liberal philosophy.

I knew that God had placed me in the galley with Lon for such a time as this. I was amazed at how God had grown me—someone who felt that she knew so little about Him and His word—to deliver apologetics. I was surprised at how calm the Holy Spirit enabled me to feel, how far God had brought my emotions when being confronted by a person with such beliefs. I was so full of God's truth that I could feel my spirit beam.

When the conversation ended, Amanda and I chatted more. We learned that we shared a couple of mutual friends. I shared how much one of them had helped me in my walk with the Lord and how grateful I was that she was so strong in Him. Throughout the trip, Amanda and I shared more and more about our lives, and we realized that we had quite a bit in common. God had surely blessed us.

How glorious it was to have another layover in Aruba. I felt I needed rest and was grateful to be in one warm, sunny place for twenty-five hours. I lounged in the afternoon sun on the beach for a while before I shopped for a swimsuit and then retired to my room. I felt I needed time alone with God. So I pulled out my Bible and prayed, and then I turned on the only Christian television network in the hotel.

The next morning, I ventured out across the beach into a cabana restaurant to order a fish sandwich. As I stood waiting to take out my lunch, I heard a voice call my name. I looked over my shoulder and spotted Amanda. She was seated at a table nearby.

As I walked over to her and sat down, I noticed that Amanda's eyes conveyed something was very wrong. "Did you hear the news?" she asked.

"What news?"

Amanda informed me that one of our commuter airplanes had crashed in Charlotte.

I felt shocked as Amanda shared how sad she was. I knew that she had worked at a commuter airline years earlier, and I assumed that she felt a particular closeness to the crew for that reason. I also knew that, as with all of us who had been in the industry for a while, she had been touched by several crashes in the past.

I shared with Amanda that when I was a gate agent, a commuter plane, onto which I had directed passengers, crashed. "I remembered their faces," I said. Amanda and I sat with our sad hearts, feeling helpless, knowing that the right thing to do was to pray. And so we did.

Afterwards, I picked up my sandwich and returned to my room and got down on my knees and prayed some more. Then I turned on cable news. There it was. The broken, blackened fragments of another airplane crashed.

How many times have I witnessed such a disaster aired on the news within my own airline? Six, I think. It was like history repeating itself, and it sickened me.

When our crew boarded the van that would transport us to the Aruba airport, the atmosphere was somber. The captain said that he didn't know anymore about the crash except that there might have been something wrong with the airplane's weight and balance.

Before passengers boarded our flight to Charlotte, I prayed again and anointed the airplane. I was surprised that none of them exhibited fear or commented on the crash. It was as if no one wanted to discuss it.

I noticed that Amanda seemed edgy, and I asked her whether she was all right. She said that the crash really bothered her. I had experienced this kind of anxiety from past crashes, so I asked her to sit down and let me serve her. I explained that after the September 11 incident, God had lifted me up to enable me to serve others in distress. I offered to pray for her. Tears filled Amanda's eyes, and we held hands.

After our prayer, I helped Amanda in the galley, offering to do anything that she didn't feel up to, including being out front serving passengers. She seemed to feel a little stronger, and so she decided to serve the people.

Much later in the flight, I walked forward and came upon Amanda speaking to a woman. I joined in their conversation and discovered that the woman worked as a gate agent for our airline. She worked the commuter flights, and her name was Hazel.

Hazel explained that she and her daughter, Rachael, had gone to Aruba to celebrate Rachael's birthday and they were on their way home. Hazel said she knew all the Charlotte-based commuter pilots. At some point, Hazel also revealed that she was a Christian. Since Amanda and Hazel both seemed to need to talk about the crash, I excused myself and returned to the coach cabin.

Later in the flight, I approached Hazel and Rachael. I asked them about their vacation and their walk with the Lord. We discovered that we had much in common. During our conversation, I shared my Christian testimony with them, not knowing exactly how God was using it until Rachael spoke up and said I had answered some of her questions. Rachael was a college student and had questioned her traditional walk with God. Included in my testimony was an explanation of how I spent years off-track searching for something greater than my circumstances before arriving at the conclusion that all I really needed was God. I suspected this was the part that helped Rachael. Hazel was delighted and graciously offered to let me stay at her house anytime while visiting Charlotte.

At the end of our flight, I recalled a woman who had pre-boarded our airplane and required oxygen throughout the flight. I went over to her and asked her if she was all right. She nodded and then explained to me that she was just released from an Aruba hospital with pneumonia. She said she and a couple of her friends had ventured down to the island for some fun and that she had gotten sick. Her friends, she said, returned to Buffalo without her. "They're supposed to pick me up," she added with a smile. She and I shared a good laugh, and I told her that I would pray for her speedy recovery.

By the time our trip was over, I felt exhilarated. God had me working plenty. I knew that He had given me a higher purpose in this mission field in the marketplace, and I never wanted to turn back.

In the break of morning, there is joy
the soaring, peaceful kind;
the quiet, floating blue and orange
extends into my mind.
With blanket clouds, it comforts me
it soothes and quiets and flows;
forever and ever, it never ends,
God's love just goes and goes.

Bibliography

Blackaby, Henry T. and Claude V. King, *Experiencing God* (Nashville: Broadman & Holman Publishers, 1994).

Brown, M.D., Rebecca and Daniel Yoder, *Unbroken Curses* (New Kensington, PA: Whitaker House, 1995).

Cherry, M.D., Reginald, *Healing Prayer* (Nashville: Thomas Nelson Publishers, 1999).

Evans, Tony, *The Battle Is the Lord's* (Chicago: Moody Press, 1998).

LaHaye, Tim and Jerry B. Jenkins, *Left Behind* (Wheaton, IL: Tyndale House Publishers, Inc., 1995).

Stanley, Charles F., *Growing Strong in Faith* audio tape series (Atlanta: In Touch Ministries, 1996).

Wilkinson, Bruce, *The Prayer of Jabez* (Sisters, OR: Multnomah Publishers, Inc., 2000).

Wilkinson, Bruce, *Secrets of the Vine* (Sisters, OR: Multnomah Publishers, Inc., 2001).

To Beth,

Your heart has been stretched beyond what most of us will ever know. I have only the greatest love, respect and admiration for you and your family. It is my fervent prayer that you will forever have divine peace amid your circumstances and that God's justice will prevail. I will remember you always.

A portion of the proceeds from

100 Passengers

will be donated to the
God's Love At Work Foundation.
This nonprofit outreach was founded by
Margaret D. Mitchell in 2005 to serve the people
of Appalachia through student scholarships and
retreat programs. To learn more about the
God's Love At Work Foundation and
Margaret D. Mitchell, visit:

www.nhffoundations.net/God'sLoveAtWork

www.MargaretDMitchell.com

P. O. Box 6906
Marietta, GA 30065-6906